Turing's Vision

Turing's Vision

The Birth of Computer Science

Chris Bernhardt

The MIT Press
Cambridge, Massachusetts
London, England

First MIT Press paperback edition, 2017
© 2016 Massachusetts Institute of Technology

This book was set in Chennai by Diacritech. Printed and bound in the United States of America.

Library of Congress Cataloging-in-Publication Data

Names: Bernhardt, Chris, author.
Title: Turing's vision : the birth of computer science / Chris Bernhardt.
Description: Cambridge, MA : The MIT Press, [2016] | Includes
    bibliographical references and index.
Identifiers: LCCN 2015039955 | ISBN 9780262034548
    (hardcover : alk. paper)—9780262533515 (paperback)
Subjects: LCSH: Turing, Alan Mathison, 1912-1954. | Computer
    engineering–Great Britain–History. | Mathematicians–Great
    Britain–Biography. | Computer algorithms–History.
Classification: LCC QA29.T8 A57 2015 | DDC 510.92–dc23 LC record
    available at http://lccn.loc.gov/2015039955

10   9

Contents

Acknowledgments

I am very grateful to a number of people for their help. Michelle Ainsworth, Denis Bell, Jonathan Fine, Chris Staecker, and three anonymous reviewers read through various drafts with extraordinary care. Their corrections and suggestions have improved the book beyond measure. I also thank Marie Lee, Kathleen Hensley, Virginia Crossman, and everyone at the MIT Press for their encouragement and help in transforming my rough proposal into this current book.

Introduction

Several biographies of his life have been published. He has been portrayed on stage by Derek Jacobi and in film by Benedict Cumberbatch. Alan Turing, if not famous, is certainly well known. Many people now know that his code breaking work during World War II played a pivotal role in the defeat of Germany. They know of his tragic death by cyanide, and perhaps of the test he devised for determining whether computers can think. Slightly less well known is the fact that the highest award in computer science is the *ACM A.M. Turing Award*. This award, often called the Nobel Prize in computing, along with a million dollars, is given annually by the Association for Computing Machinery for outstanding contributions to computer science. The ACM named the award after Turing because he is considered as one of the founders of computer science. But why? What did he do to help found computer science? The answer is that he wrote a remarkable paper in 1936, when he was just twenty four years old. This paper is Turing's most important intellectual contribution. However, this paper and its groundbreaking ideas are not widely known. This book is about that paper.

The paper has the rather uninviting title, *On Computable Numbers, with an Application to the Entscheidungsproblem*. But don't be discouraged by the title, because it contains a wealth of elegant and powerful results. It also contains some remarkably beautiful proofs. Turing wants to show that a leading mathematician's view of mathematics is wrong. To do this he needs to study computation: What exactly is computation? How can we define it? Are there problems that cannot be solved by computation? He answers these questions with dazzling skill and creativity.

Turing thinks carefully about how humans perform computations. He realizes that any computation can be broken down to a sequence of simple steps. Then he constructs theoretical machines capable of performing each of these steps. These machines, which we now call Turing machines, are capable of doing any computation.[1] After this, he shows that you don't need a different machine for each different algorithm, you can design one machine that can compute any algorithm. In the process he invents the stored-program concept, which as we will see is crucial to the development of modern computers. Finally, he proves that there are certain problems that are beyond any computer's power to solve.

Turing machines are theoretical models of our modern computers. Everything that can be computed on a computer can be computed by a Turing machine, so his paper is not just of historical interest; it tells us about what can and cannot be computed by any computer. It tells us that there are limitations to computation, and that there are simple questions that at first glance look straightforward, but are beyond the power of any computer to answer correctly.

The ideas contained in the paper are now taught at the undergraduate level, typically in a course called *Theory of Computation*. However, most university students don't take the course and so don't come across Turing's work. In general, a very small proportion of the population knows what Turing did in this paper. This is a pity considering that the work both contains some extraordinary ideas and is relevant to our modern life.

General relativity and quantum mechanics were also both developed during the first half of the twentieth century. Most people have an idea, if rather hazy, of what these theories say. Part of the difficulty in really understanding these two theories is that they are based on sophisticated mathematics. This is not the case with Turing's work. As Marvin Minsky writes, "The sheer simplicity of the theory's foundation and extraordinarily short path from this foundation to its logical and surprising conclusions give the theory a mathematical beauty that alone guarantees it a permanent place in computer theory."[2]

The aim of this book is to do exactly what Minsky describes. We begin with the foundations and build to Turing's surprising conclusions, but we also try to place Turing's work in context. To do this, some of the history that lead up to Turing's paper and some of the history that followed afterwards is given.

There have been many people with many views of computation, and there is no right or wrong view. Different views can reveal remarkably different vistas. We will pause along the way to look at some of these. In particular, one completely different way of looking at computation was developed by the Princeton logician Alonzo Church. Both Church and Turing were working to give an answer to a challenge posed by David Hilbert. Both came to the same conclusion, that the implicit assumption that Hilbert was making was wrong, but Church published the result first. Turing was still working on his paper when he discovered and read Church's paper — he must have been bitterly disappointed to know that someone else had reached the same conclusion and beaten him to publication. However, they had tackled the problem in different ways, and their proofs were substantially different. Turing's argument was remarkably simple and elegant. His paper was not published for the result, but for the proof of the result.

Mathematicians often describe proofs in terms of beauty. When doing mathematics there is an aesthetic that guides. At times you have a proof, but feel that it is clumsy and that there must be a better one that needs to be found. This is what the Hungarian mathematician Paul Erdős was referring to when he talked about *The Book*. According to Erdős, there is a book in which God had written down all the shortest, most beautiful proofs. Erdős famously said "You don't have to believe in God, but you should believe in *The Book*." Turing's proofs, along with those of Gödel and Georg Cantor on which they are based, are definitely in *The Book*.

This book is for the reader who wants to understand these ideas. We start from the beginning and build carefully. The reader doesn't have to know much mathematics — high school provides enough — but it does require some mathematical aptitude and also a little work. It needs to be read carefully, and some sections may need to be re-read. This is to be expected since Turing is not saying trivial things about computation, but saying deep and nonintuitive things. That said, many people find these ideas quite fascinating and the work rewarding.

Here is a brief outline of some of the main ideas and the order in which we will meet them.

Chapter 1

This chapter looks at some of the history of mathematics in the second half of the nineteenth century and the beginning of the twentieth. It describes how the foundations of mathematics seemed somewhat shaky and how various people tried to secure them. One of these mathematicians was David Hilbert, who as part of his program, stated the "Entscheidungsprobem" (Decision Problem, in English). The problem concerns finding algorithms for deciding whether certain general statements in mathematics are true or false. Hilbert was certain that such algorithms existed.

This led to the question of what it meant to perform a computation. Computation had always been part of mathematics. In fact for centuries mathematics and computation were essentially synonymous, but now there was a shift. Instead of computation being solely a tool, it became a topic of study in its own right.

Turing's goal in writing his paper was to prove that Hilbert's view of the power of computation was wrong.

Chapter 2

Turing wanted to show that there were problems that were beyond any computer's ability to solve. In particular, he wanted to find a decision problem that he could prove was undecidable. The goal of this chapter is to explain what the terms *decision problem* and *undecidable* mean and why they are important.

We look at three well-known decision problems that have been proven to be undecidable, and examine what undecidability means in these cases.

Chapter 3

Turing defined computation in terms of theoretical computing machines. We begin our study of automata — theoretical computing machines — by studying the finite case. These are simpler than Turing machines, and so are easier to describe and to work with. We look at what they can compute and also give some examples of questions that we show are beyond their power. We also see how computations by these automata are related to Post's correspondence problem, an undecidable decision problem, which we looked at in the previous chapter.

Regular expressions are introduced and their equivalence to finite automata explained. We begin to see that having more than one description of computation can be helpful.

Chapter 4

This chapter introduces Turing machines. These don't seem much more complicated than finite automata, but turn out to be much more powerful. The examples from the previous chapter that were beyond finite automata are shown to be able to be handled by these new machines.

The Church-Turing Thesis, that any algorithm whatsoever can be implemented by a Turing machine, is described.

We also see that these machines introduce an important new phenomenon, some machines never halt on their input. They run forever.

Chapter 5

In addition to Turing's approach, there are several different ways at looking at computation. In this chapter we pause to examine at three of these. We begin with the lambda calculus (λ-calculus) of Alonzo Church, then look at an example of a tag system, finally we consider cellular automata.

These views of computation seem very different, but each perspective has its own strengths. The λ-calculus leads to programming languages; tag systems are useful for proving different systems equivalent; cellular automata give pictures of complete computations. After this brief detour we return to Turing's arguments.

Chapter 6

Up until now, machines have been described by diagrams. This chapter starts by showing how finite automata and Turing machines can be described by finite sequences of digits, called *encodings*. It is analogous to high-level programs being converted into machine language.

Encodings lead to the idea of Universal Turing machines — a machine that can input both a program and data and then run the program on the data. We see that modern computers are universal machines.

Chapter 7

The final topic of the previous chapter concerned running machines on finite sequences of digits that correspond to the description of the machines, that is, running machines on their encodings. This self-referential idea is extremely important. We examine it in detail and show that it leads to proofs that certain problems are undecidable.

It is not assumed that the reader has a strong mathematical background. In this and the next chapter proofs by contradiction are needed. The chapter starts with an explanation of this method of proof — the classical proof that the square root of two is not rational is carefully presented. Then Russell's *Barber Paradox* is described.

After these introductory ideas, the arguments return to automata. It is shown that there are some finite automata that accept their encodings and some that do not, but there is no finite automaton that can distinguish these two classes.

This idea is then extended to Turing machines: there are some Turing machines that accept their encodings and some that do not, but there is no Turing machine that can distinguish these two classes. This, in turn, leads to the the proofs that certain decision problems are undecidable. In particular, we prove that the *halting problem* and the *acceptance problem* are both undecidable.

Chapter 8

The title of Turing's paper is *On Computable Numbers, with an Application to the Entscheidungsproblem*. The connection to the Entscheidungsproblem has now been explained, but computable numbers have not. In this chapter we explain what these numbers are and the basic result concerning them.

The chapter starts with Cantor's idea of cardinality. We look at some basic, but surprising facts, about infinite cardinal numbers. Cantor's diagonal and general arguments for showing two sets have different cardinalities are given.

We then return to Turing's paper. Computable numbers are defined. We also explain what it means to be effectively enumerable. We conclude by giving Turing's proof that computable numbers are not effectively enumerable.

Chapter 9

The final chapter describes both what happened to Turing and the computer in the years after his paper was published.

It begins with Turing going to Princeton to obtain his Ph.D. under Church. This is where he gets to know John von Neumann. It then describes Turing's move back to England and his work during the Second World War on code breaking.

After this, we briefly look at how the modern computer came into existence during the forties. The procession from sophisticated calculator, to universal computer, to stored-program universal computer is outlined. In particular, we note that the stored-program concept originates with Turing's paper.

In 1950, Turing published a paper with a description of what is now called the Turing Test. This and the subsequent history of the idea are briefly described.

The chapter ends with Jack Copeland's recent study of Turing's death and the fact that it might have been accidental, and not suicide. We conclude with the text of Gordon Brown's apology on behalf of the British government.

1 Background

"Mathematics, rightly viewed, possesses not only truth, but supreme beauty — a beauty cold and austere, like that of sculpture, without appeal to any part of our weaker nature, without the gorgeous trappings of painting or music, yet sublimely pure, and capable of a stern perfection such as only the greatest art can show."
Bertrand Russell[1]

In 1935, at the age of 22, Alan Turing was elected a Fellow at King's College, Cambridge. He had just finished his undergraduate degree in mathematics. He was bright and ambitious. As an undergraduate he had proved the *Central Limit Theorem*, probably the most fundamental result in statistics. This theorem explains the ubiquity of the normal distribution and why it occurs in so many guises. However, though Turing had given a proof, it was quickly pointed out to him that he was not the first to do so. Jarl Waldemar Lindeberg had published a proof of the theorem over a decade earlier. Though Turing's argument was not pioneering, it did show that he had real talent and great potential. It was enough to get him elected as a Fellow: a position that provided money, board and lodging for three years with the only requirement that he would concentrate on mathematical research. Now he had to prove himself. He had to do something original. What better way than to tackle a problem of the world's leading mathematician and prove him wrong? This is exactly what Turing set out to do. He would tackle Hilbert's *Entscheidungsproblem*.

Before we describe what Turing did, it is helpful to understand why Hilbert stated his problem. This requires introducing some of developments in mathematics that occurred during the second half of the nineteenth century and first part of the twentieth century. In particular, we will look at the rise of mathematical logic, the attempts to find a firm axiomatic foundation for mathematics, and the role of algorithms.

Mathematical Certainty

Mathematics is often seen as the epitome of certainty. If we can't be certain of mathematical truths can we be certain of anything? However, in the history of mathematics there have been times when it looked as though the foundations were not secure and that the whole structure might collapse. Perhaps the first time that this feeling of uncertainty in mathematics occurred was in the fifth century BCE and, according to legend, resulted in the murder of Hippasus of Metapontum for proving a theorem. We don't have a record of his proof, but it seems probable that it is a version of what is now regarded as one of the most beautiful proofs in mathematics. (We will see the full proof later.)

The ancient Greek number system consisted of whole numbers and ratios of whole numbers or what nowadays are called the integers and the rational numbers. Hippasus considered a right triangle with base and height both of length one. He then showed that the length of the hypotenuse was not a rational number. From the modern viewpoint this is not a problem. In addition to the rational numbers, we have numbers like π and e that are irrational. We can interpret Hippasus's argument as showing that $\sqrt{2}$ is an irrational number. However, for the Greeks there was a real problem. They only had the rational numbers. For them, Hippasus's argument showed that the length of the hypotenuse could not be a number, and consequently that some lengths were not numbers.

Hippasus was a Pythagorean. The Pythagoreans were a mystical sect that believed that numbers showed the underlying nature of all things. To have one of their members prove that some lengths could not have numbers assigned to them must have been extremely disturbing — it challenged their fundamental belief. The legend is that when Hippasus showed his proof to the other Pythagoreans, they killed the messenger. They wrapped him in chains, rowed to the middle of a lake and drowned him. This story may or may not be true, but the discovery of incommensurable lengths undoubtedly caused the first seismic shift in mathematics.

Numbers seem to be basic objects, but so do lengths. Clearly, you can draw a right triangle with base and height of length one and it has a hypotenuse. The hypotenuse has a length, but strangely, if you are an ancient Greek, you cannot assign a number to this length. Arguments of this type led the Greeks to feel that lengths were the more fundamental objects. Numbers seemed a little worrisome — a little less certain. Number theory had initially seemed to be the most basic and certain of the mathematical sciences, but this changed and now geometry took its place.

Since this time, up to the present, geometry has remained an important part of mathematics education. The reason for this is due largely to one man and one book — Euclid and his *Elements*. In the *Elements*, Euclid constructed both an encyclopedia of known mathematics and a textbook. This text has been actively studied since it was originally written — an era of more than two millennia. It was known to both the Byzantine and Arab mathematicians. The first printed edition was in 1482 and it has been in print ever since.

Euclid started with a list of axioms, or postulates,[2] and then derived subsequent results from them. Each new theorem could be deduced using logic from the axioms and previous deductions.

The axiomatic approach gives the impression of mathematical certainty. If we know that our initial axioms are true, and we know our logical deductions are valid, then we can be sure about our conclusions. The problem is that it is very easy to make unwarranted assumptions — assumptions that might seem obvious and might even be true, but that cannot be deduced from the initial axioms. As unwarranted assumptions gradually slip into proofs, the logical validity vanishes and the mathematical certainty is lost.

By the nineteenth century, it was realized that there were many places where Euclid was making assumptions that did not come from his postulates. There needed to be a revision. The statements that Euclid was incorporating into his proofs that couldn't be derived from the axioms would have to be added to his list of axioms. The whole framework needed to be both expanded and updated.

David Hilbert took up the challenge. In 1899 he published his *Grundlagen der Geometrie* (Foundations of Geometry) in which he gave a new, longer, and complete list of axioms. Hilbert was very careful to make sure that unjustified assumptions did not creep into proofs. To achieve this, his perspective on axioms was very different from Euclid's.

For Euclid, an axiom such as *two distinct points define a unique straight line* was a self-evident truth. Points and lines had a meaning attached to them. Hilbert's approach differed. Hilbert realized that any system of axioms and definitions would have to start somewhere and these starting statements would have to contain terms that had not been defined earlier.

For Hilbert, an axiom was a statement that you could use to prove other statements, but you should not think of it as a self-evident truth. The axiom *two distinct points define a unique straight line* contains the words "point" and "line." These are undefined concepts and so should have no meaning attached to them. The axioms then define relations between the undefined concepts. As Hilbert pointed out, since undefined terms had no meaning attached, you could replace "point" and "line" by any other words. He is said to have given an example in which "points," "lines," and "planes" were replaced with the words "tables," "chairs," and "glasses of beer."

Bertrand Russell famously summed up the situation, somewhat facetiously, by asserting, "Mathematics may be defined as the subject where we never know what we are talking about, nor whether what we are saying is true."[3] Of course, we do want the terms "points" and "lines" to tell us things about what we normally think about when we talk of points and lines, but Hilbert was making the point that any proof involving these terms should be derivable only from the axioms and not from statements that come from our visualizations of the terms.

It now looked as though geometry was back on a secure axiomatic footing. Hilbert's success with geometry naturally led to the question of whether the axiomatic method could be applied to the whole of mathematics. Could a list of axioms be found from which all of mathematics could be constructed? A number of people, including Hilbert and Russell, thought that this axiomatic approach should be possible. But before we look at what Russell, Hilbert, and others did, we need to talk a little about the development of mathematical logic.

Boole's Logic

Logic has always been part of mathematics. Indeed, part of the reason the *Elements* was so influential, especially in education, was the approach that Euclid took. It was not just a list of mathematical results, but contained the logical arguments that showed how these results could be obtained from simpler ones. It was a text that not only taught you mathematics, but also taught you how to argue logically, and to be truly educated you had to have some acquaintance with these arguments. Abraham Lincoln notably wrote: "At last I said, — Lincoln, you never can make a lawyer if you do not understand what demonstrate means; and I left my situation in Springfield, went home to my father's house, and stayed there till I could give any proposition in the six books of Euclid at sight. I then found out what demonstrate means, and went back to my law studies."[4]

Logic had always been used for mathematical arguments, but in the nineteenth century it became an area of mathematical study in its own right. This new approach began with George Boole, who realized that algebra could be applied to part of logic. Certain logical deductions involving statements using the connectives "and," "or," and "not' could be reduced to algebraic manipulation of symbols.

He first published his results in 1847, but then polished them into final form for his book *An investigation into the Laws of Thought on Which are Founded the Mathematical Theories of Logic and Probabilities* which he published in 1854.

Boole's results were extended by other mathematicians to form what is now known as Boolean algebra. This algebra is important to our story because it is both the start of mathematical logic and the basis for the design of computers. (In the notes we give an example using Boolean algebra that shows that saying "it is Saturday *or* it is raining" is *not true* is equivalent to saying that "it is *not* Saturday *and* it is *not* raining" is *true*.)[5]

Mathematical Logic

Boole's algebra dealt only with what is now called *propositional logic* or *zeroth-order logic*. It didn't include *quantifiers* like "all" and "some." Statements such as "some positive integers are primes" and "all integers are rational numbers" cannot be dealt with at this level.

The next step was to extend Boole's approach to include quantifiers, and consequently convert all of the logic needed for mathematics into algebraic form, where all the logical arguments could be performed by symbolic manipulation. This was done independently by Charles Sanders Peirce in America and Gottlob Frege in Germany. Frege published his results on quantifiers first, but Peirce's work was more influential to the subsequent development of mathematical logic. This was partly because of his superior notation, but mainly due to the work of another German mathematician, Ernst Schröder, who wrote the influential and widely used textbook on mathematical logic that explained and expanded on the work of both Boole and Peirce.[6]

Once it was shown that logic had a mathematical structure, it raised the question of whether machines could be constructed for doing logical computations. Before we continue with our discussion of the foundations of mathematics, we will take a brief digression to introduce a couple of people who constructed machines.

Logic machines

William Stanley Jevons, the English economist and logician, was one of the first to realize that Boolean logic could be handled by a machine. He built his *Logic Piano* to compute small truth tables. It had keys, like a piano, that were used for inputting the initial premisses. It was built in 1869 and went on display at the Royal Society in 1870.[7] The Logic Piano was not practically useful because it could only deal with simple cases that were easily done by hand, but it showed that machines could do logic.

Allan Marquand, who had been a student of Peirce, constructed his *Logical Machine* in 1882 at Princeton, where he was teaching logic and Latin. The machine, like Jevons's, was quite limited in what it could do. Peirce wrote to him suggesting that a more advanced machine be constructed using electromechanics. However, around this time the President of Princeton decided that Peirce's mathematical approach to logic was "unorthodox and unCalvinistic" and that it would be better if Marquand stopped teaching logic and switched to art history. Marquand became a successful art historian, but his work in logic ceased.

It was also around this time that Peirce married his second wife, and it was discovered that he had been living with her before they were married.

The resulting scandal ended his academic career. He was fired from his position at Johns Hopkins University and no other university would employ him. It was a sad ending for someone that Russell described as "...one of the most original minds of the later nineteenth century, and certainly the greatest American thinker ever."

Securing the Foundations of Mathematics

Frege's work caught the interest of Bertrand Russell. Russell was not so much interested in how Frege had developed logic, but for his view of how logic related to mathematics. Frege was one of the founders of the idea of *logicism*; the idea that logic forms the foundation of mathematics. According to this philosophy, first one develops logic and then mathematics should be constructed from the logic. Everything would be built upon precise rules. Frege spent many years developing his theory, but, unfortunately, just as he was about to publish the second volume of his work, in which he outlined the approach in detail, he received a letter from Russell that pointed out a fundamental flaw. Frege had developed his theory from sets, which he had taken to be synonymous with collections. He hadn't realized that this seemingly simple idea could cause problems.

Russell understood that sets had to be defined more carefully. Frege's formulation allowed you to consider the set of all possible sets — the largest possible set — and this led to paradoxes. Russell contacted Frege explaining the problem. Frege hurriedly added a postscript to his book saying, "Hardly anything more unfortunate can befall a scientific writer than to have one of the foundations of his edifice shaken after the work was finished. This was the position I was placed in by the letter of Mr. Bertrand Russell, just when printing of this volume was nearing its completion." But though Russell had essentially demolished Frege's work, he thought Frege had the right approach. Frege's work could be redone.

This is what he attempted to do in his most important mathematical work — the massive *Principia Mathematica* — written with Alfred North Whitehead. It was an endeavor to build mathematics from the foundations. As with Frege's approach, the start was logic and from logic they moved on to arithmetic. However, it was incredibly slow going. After three volumes (published in 1910, 1912, 1913) they had only got up to real numbers. To give some idea of the amount of detail that went into making sure no unwarranted assumptions were creeping in, and the consequent length of the arguments, it wasn't until the three hundred and sixty second page, about half way through the first volume, that one finds the statement: "From this proposition it will follow, when arithmetical addition has been defined, that $1 + 1 = 2$." Arithmetical addition didn't get defined in this volume, but had to wait for the second.

Even the authors were surprised at how lengthy the enterprise was turning out to be. They had written three volumes and they were nowhere near the end. The next volume was supposed to be on geometry, but Russell and Whitehead, seeing the immensity of what would be needed, decided to abandon the project at this point.

It is a monumental piece of work of about two thousand pages, some of these pages contain nothing but symbols, but there are also eloquent descriptions of what is being done and why — Russell was an excellent writer. Even though the project was never completed, the published work was influential, and not only in mathematical circles. Its emphasis on clarity and care with language attracted a much wider audience. T. S. Eliot, a great admirer of the work, commented: "How much the work of logicians has done to make of English a language in which it is possible to think clearly and exactly on any subject. The *Principia Mathematica* are perhaps a greater contribution to our language than they are to mathematics."[8]

Hilbert's Approach

In addition to mathematical logic, the nineteenth century also saw the creation of the study of non-Euclidean geometries. These were geometries that were constructed using all the axioms for Euclidean geometry with the exception of the axiom concerning parallel lines. Various theorems were proved in these geometries that were strikingly different from their Euclidean counterparts. Questions arose as to whether these axiom systems might eventually lead to paradoxes. Could we be sure that given a set of axioms that they were *consistent*, that it was not possible to prove a statement both true and false? Could the axioms of non-Euclidean geometries lead to paradoxes? Were we even sure that the axioms of Euclidean geometry did not contain contradictions? To try to answer questions like these, models of one area of mathematics were developed within another.

Hilbert showed that Euclidean geometry was consistent if arithmetic was consistent. Proofs were given that non-Euclidean geometries were consistent if Euclidean geometry was. These proofs of relative consistency were comforting, but it was realized that a proof of consistency shouldn't depend on the assumption that another area of mathematics was consistent. It really needed to start with an area that one could prove was consistent. This led Hilbert to list the basic properties that he felt that the axiomatic foundations of mathematics should have.

The first property was that the axioms should be *consistent*. The axioms should never lead to paradoxes — there should be no statements that could be proved to be both true and false. But more than this, there should be a proof that the axioms are consistent. The proof should not involve ideas that were not provable from the axioms. It should be provable from the axioms — from within the system.

The second property was that the axioms should be *complete*. Every statement in mathematics should be able to be either proved or disproved from the axioms.

These ideas that mathematics should be built on a system of axioms that were complete, consistent and had a proof of consistency from within the system became known as *Hilbert's Program*. Hilbert proposed the original program in 1920. In 1928, he explicitly added the Entscheidungsproblem. This was another property he thought mathematics should have. There should be a *decision procedure* that will tell us whether a statement can be proved from the axioms. By decision procedure, Hilbert meant a clear computational process, what we now call an *algorithm*,[9] that would start with the axioms and a potential conclusion and would then tell us whether the potential conclusion could be proved from the axioms. Hilbert was certain that such an algorithm existed. The Entscheidungsproblem was the problem of finding the algorithm.

Though Hilbert liked the idea of this orderly and mechanical approach to mathematics others did not. The English mathematician G. H. Hardy, in particular, was convinced that Hilbert was wrong. He said of the Entscheidungsproblem in 1928, "There is of course no such theorem, and this is very fortunate, since if there were we should have a mechanical set of rules for the solution of all mathematical problems, and our activities as mathematicians would come to an end." [10]

Hilbert disagreed with Hardy. He was convinced that the algorithm existed, that every problem in mathematics could be solved, and that in each case there should be an algorithm that would give the solution. He famously said: "Wir müssen wissen. Wir werden wissen." In English: "We must know. We will know." When he died these words were inscribed on his tombstone. He was certain that his program would give a secure framework from which all of mathematics could be built.

However, this was not to be. Even before the end of his life, his program was shown to be unworkable in its totality. First there were the results of Gödel, and then the results of Church and Turing.

Gödel's Results

In 1931, the Austrian logician, Kurt Gödel, published a landmark paper titled *Über formal unentscheidbare Sätze der "Principia Mathematica" und verwandter Systeme* ("On Formally Undecidable Propositions of "Principia Mathematica" and Related Systems"). In this paper he looked at systems of axioms that were strong enough to prove results about numbers — Russell and Whitehead's *Principia Mathematica* being the prototypical example of such a system. Gödel showed that if the axioms were consistent, then they could not be complete. There would be statements that could be neither proven nor disproven from the axioms. He also showed that it was impossible to prove the consistency of the axioms from within the system.

Gödel had completely destroyed Hilbert's program as it stood in 1920. Nevertheless, there was still the Entscheidungsproblem.

Turing's Results

This was the situation as Turing started his fellowship at Cambridge. In the spring of 1935, he had attended a course given by Max Newman on the foundations of mathematics in which Newman explained Gödel's results. It was here that Turing learned of the Entscheidungsproblem. He determined to show that Hilbert was wrong. Hilbert was asking for the construction of an algorithm. He was making the implicit assumption that an algorithm existed. Turing would show that this implicit assumption was wrong. He would show that there were questions that were beyond the power of algorithms to answer. He would construct a proof showing that Hardy was correct — a proof that there was no mechanical set of rules for the solutions of all mathematical problems and consequently that our activities as mathematicians would never come to an end.

Hilbert hadn't given a formal definition of what he meant by decision procedure. He might not have felt the need for several reasons. Historically, mathematics was identified with computation — the term *mathematics* referred to astronomy and astrology, and the calculation of star and planet locations.[11] Until the nineteenth century proofs were essentially computational. Most mathematicians were involved in either developing or using algorithms for explicit computations — using algorithms was an intrinsic part of doing mathematics. However, questions like Hilbert's Entscheidungsproblem began to lead some mathematicians and logicians to ask "What exactly is a computation?" and "What is the definition of an algorithm?"

If Turing was going to give a mathematical proof showing that certain algorithms did not exist, then he needed to answer these questions. Others would give their answers, including the logicians Gödel and Alonzo Church, but Turing's fresh insight was to define algorithms in terms of theoretical computing machines. Later we will look at various approaches to computation, and I think that the elegant simplicity of Turing's approach will become clear.

The second step of his argument was to take his machines and convert them into strings of numbers. This can be compared to taking programs that are written in a high-level programming language and converting them into strings of binary digits, machine code, for the actual computer to work on. Nowadays we know that computers work with binary strings and that we interact with them using ordinary language. It is clear that there must be a way of converting our instructions into binary. But in the 1930s the idea of converting instructions to strings of binary numbers was highly innovative. Computers at this time meant people who did computations, not machines, and human computers expected to get their instructions in everyday English, not as a string of 0s and 1s.

Now that Turing had algorithms written as strings of numbers, he could describe a Universal Computer. This is a computer that can take both an algorithm and data as input and then run the algorithm on the data. This is an extremely important idea. A universal Turing machine can simulate any other Turing machine. Consequently, a universal Turing machine can do any computation that can be done by any other Turing machine — it can run any algorithm.

All modern computers are stored-program computers — where the data and programs are treated in exactly the same way. This idea originated with Turing. As we progress through Turing's argument we will be doing computations. We will be computers. At some point we will see how to decode a string of digits into two components, an algorithm and data to be run by the algorithm. We will be universal computers. In fact we have been universal computers ever since the age we could follow instructions. We will see that not only are we universal computers, but we have the computational power equivalent to the most powerful supercomputer that exists or will exist in the future.

Universal computers are important, but Turing did more with his encoding of algorithms into strings of digits. He wanted to show that there were problems that initially looked tractable, but were completely beyond the power of any computer. To do this he borrowed another argument from Gödel who, in turn, had borrowed it from Cantor. This was Cantor's generalized diagonal argument.

This, in a nutshell, was Turing's approach to giving a negative answer to the Entscheidungsproblem. It is an incredibly beautiful argument with many interlocking ideas. We will look at this argument in detail, carefully going through each step.

Turing's paper can be viewed two ways. It is a paper on the logical foundations of mathematics that helped to end Hilbert's program by showing that the Entscheidungsproblem was fundamentally flawed. But it is also the paper that started the study of the theory of computation and computer science. It can be viewed as the ending of one era and the start of another. Viewing it the first way, puts the emphasis on statements in logic. Viewing it the second way, puts the emphasis on running programs. At the time the paper was written, Turing clearly viewed it the first way. When these ideas are taught today, it makes more sense to relate them to current computers and so we tend to view them the second way.

Though I have stressed the elegance of Turing's paper, it is actually quite a difficult paper to read. Students today are presented with a modern and more simplified version of Turing's ideas. In 1958, Martin Davis published a book *Computability and Unsolvability* that was based on a course he taught at the University of Illinois. In 1967, Marvin Minsky, co-founder of the M.I.T.'s Artificial Intelligence laboratory, published *Computation: Finite and Infinite Machines* based on a course at M.I.T. These books were extremely influential, presenting Turing's ideas in a way that was much easier to comprehend, and led to the study of the theory of computation as a part of computer science and to computer science becoming its own discipline. Much of the modern approach follows from these two authors. For example, nowadays the decision problem that concerned Turing is usually presented after the much easier to explain *halting problem*, which first appeared in Davis's book. We will take this modern approach to describe Turing's work.

None of the fundamental ideas are changed, but there is a different perspective. We are not so much interested in what numbers a computer can compute, than in what programs a computer can run. We want to ask questions and see if there is an algorithm, or a program, that will answer the question. Turing's proof of the Entscheidungsproblem becomes a question of showing that certain decision problems are undecidable.

Undecidability is a key idea in Turing's paper, and it is a good place to start our study of his ideas. In the next chapter we will look at some examples of undecidable decision problems and see a little more clearly what this term really means.

2 Some Undecidable Decision Problems

In this chapter we will look at three undecidable decision problems. All are famous problems. One is Hilbert's tenth problem, another is Post's correspondence problem and the third is the halting problem. But first, let us describe exactly what it means for a problem to be a decision problem.

We will start with an easy example. Consider the question: *Given two positive integers x and y, is $x^2 + y^2$ the square of a positive integer?* The answer to the question obviously depends on what values are chosen for x and y. If we choose $x = 3$ and $y = 4$, then $x^2 + y^2 = 9 + 16 = 25$, which is 5 squared, so the answer to the question, in this particular case, is yes. If we input $x = 1$ and $y = 1$, then $x^2 + y^2 = 2$, and we know that 2 is not the square of an integer, so the answer, in this case, is no. Given particular values of the input parameters, the question has an answer of either *yes* or *no*. This is exactly what a decision problem is. It is a question that depends on input parameters. Once the input parameters are chosen, it becomes a yes/no question.

A decision problem is *decidable* if it is possible to construct an algorithm, or equivalently a computer program, that gives the correct answer in every case. The problem is *undecidable* if it is not possible to construct an algorithm that can answer the question correctly in every case.

Our example of asking whether $x^2 + y^2$ is the square of a positive integer is an example of a decidable decision problem. It is easy to write a program that takes x and y as input and tells us whether or not $x^2 + y^2$ is a perfect square.

To show that a decision problem is undecidable is often very difficult. It is not enough to work for some time and be unable to devise an algorithm that answers the problem. To show that a problem is undecidable, you have to *prove* that no such algorithm exists. Proofs showing something doesn't exist are often much harder than proofs showing that something exists. A straightforward way of showing something exists is to find a concrete example of the thing you are looking for, but it is usually far from straightforward to prove non-existence. You have to show that it is impossible to find an example.

Below, we will describe problems that are known to be undecidable. We will describe them in detail and discuss what the fact that they are undecidable says about them. We leave until later chapters the ideas that underly the proofs of undecidability.

We begin by looking at Post's correspondence problem, but first we introduce this important figure in the theory of computation.

Emil Post

In 1920, Emil Post was a graduate student at Columbia University completing his Ph.D. In his dissertation he looked at Russell and Whitehead's *Principia* and showed that axioms underlying the zeroth-order logic — the propositional calculus — were both consistent and complete. (It is not until the axioms for numbers are added that the problems with consistency and completeness occur.) After graduation he moved to a one-year post-doctoral position at Princeton. His goal was to study all of the axioms contained in the *Principia* with the hope of also proving them complete and consistent.

His approach led him to look at what he called *tag systems*. (We will introduce them later in the book.) He showed that the axioms in *Principia* could in theory be reduced to a simpler form, called normal forms, that resembled his tag systems. He realized that proofs for results from the axioms of the *Principia* could be reduced to simple operations on strings of symbols.

His research was both highly original and groundbreaking. He had essentially discovered the main ideas underlying both Gödel's Incompleteness Theorem and the disproof of the Entscheidungsproblem. Post was working in this area in 1921. Gödel published his result in 1931, Church and Turing published their results in 1936, so Post was ten years ahead of them. Unfortunately he didn't publish any of this work. Post was bipolar and had his first attack in 1921. For the rest of his life he would have to be periodically hospitalized and given electroshock — the standard treatment at the time.[1] After his first hospitalization he worked with his doctor to determine what he could and could not do to prevent further manic attacks. He limited the amount of mathematical research he could do during the day, working on two problems at once so that if one problem became too stimulating he could switch to the other. He had tremendous support from his wife and family who were extremely devoted to him. But even so, he still didn't publish anything until 1930.

In 1935 he joined the faculty at City College of New York where he worked until the end of his life. During this time his earlier work became known and he continued to be both productive and highly innovative. The University of Chicago mathematician, Robert Soare, writes, "As Turing left the subject of pure computability theory in 1939, his mantle fell on Post. Post continued the tradition of clear, intuitive proofs, of exploring the most basic objects such as computability and computably enumerable (c.e.) sets, and most of all, exploring relative computability and Turing reducibility. During the next decade and a half, from 1940 until his death in 1954, Post played an extraordinary role in shaping the subject."

In 1946 Post published his correspondence problem. We will describe it because it is an example of an undecidable problem that is very easy to state.

Post's Correspondence Problem

Imagine that a catalog lists various type of tiles. Each tile in the catalog has a design consisting of two sequences of 1s and 2s, with one sequence above the other. You are allowed to order as many tiles of each of the various types as you like. The goal is to find a collection of tiles that when lined up side-by-side has the entire top sequence of 1s and 2s equal to the bottom sequence. To illustrate we will look at two examples of catalogs.

The first catalog
The first catalog has the three types of tiles depicted below.

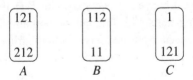

$$A \qquad B \qquad C$$

121	112	1
212	11	121

We are now allowed to choose as many of each type of tile as we want (including zero, but we must choose at least one tile of some type), and then we have to then line them up so that the top sequence is equal to the bottom sequence.

In this case, a solution to the correspondence problem is given by choosing four tiles, one A, one C and two Bs and then arranging them in the order $BABC$

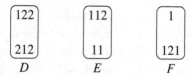

This ordering has the sequence 1121211121 along both the bottom and the top, so we have a solution for this particular catalog.

We will now look at another catalog for which there is no solution.

The second catalog
Again the catalog has three types of tiles:

$$
\begin{array}{ccc}
\boxed{\begin{array}{c} 122 \\ \hline 212 \end{array}} & \boxed{\begin{array}{c} 112 \\ \hline 11 \end{array}} & \boxed{\begin{array}{c} 1 \\ \hline 121 \end{array}} \\
D & E & F
\end{array}
$$

We will try to construct a solution — carefully going through all possible steps. We will start with the leftmost tile, then proceed by adding tiles to the right.

It is clear that we cannot start with D as the leftmost tile because if we did the top string would start with 1 and the bottom with 2.

We will see what happens if we start with E as the first tile. In this case, the top string starts with 112 and the bottom with 11. To obtain a solution we now need a tile that has a bottom string starting with a 2. Consequently we are forced to use tile D next. Looking at ED, we see that we have 112122 on top and 11212 on the bottom, so, as before, we need a tile with a bottom string starting with a 2 as our next tile. Once again we are forced to pick D. We now have EDD. This has 112122122 on top and 11212212 on the bottom. Again we need a tile with a bottom string starting with a 2. Yet again it has to be another D — and the process repeats. At each stage we are forced to add one more D on the right, but we will never reach a solution as at each stage the top string will be one digit longer than the bottom string. This tells us that there cannot be a solution that starts with E.

We have seen that we cannot obtain a solution that starts with either D or E as the leftmost tile. The only other possibility is starting with F. In this case, the top string starts with 1 and the bottom with 121. For a solution we need a tile with a top string that starts with a 2. Unfortunately, there isn't one. Consequently, there is no solution that starts with F. Since we have considered all possible starting tiles and ruled each one out, we know that there cannot be a solution for this particular catalog.

Given any catalog of tiles, there are these two possibilities. Either there is a solution to the correspondence problem or there isn't. Given a catalog, we would like a procedure that could tell us whether there is or is not a solution to the problem. Post showed that this decision problem was undecidable. This means that there is no algorithm, or equivalently computer program, that can take as input catalogs of tiles and, for each catalog, tell us whether or not there is a solution to the correspondence problem. This is a stunning result! It doesn't say that no one has found an algorithm that works. It says that there is no such algorithm. It cannot exist.

We will look at this in a little more detail and study its consequences by actually constructing an algorithm that looks as though it might work and then use the fact that by Post's result we know no such algorithm exists to conclude that it cannot.

An algorithm

Here is an algorithm that we will call Algorithm I: Given any catalog with a finite number of tiles, first see if there is any one tile that is a solution to the correspondence problem. If there is a tile, we don't have to do any more work, we have our solution. If there is no one tile that solves the problem, try all possible combinations of two tiles. If there is a solution with two tiles we will find it. If no combination of two tiles solves the problem, try all possible combinations of three tiles — and so on.

If we try the algorithm on our first catalog we would begin by seeing whether any of A, B or C give a solution. Since none do, we would see if any of AA, AB, AC, BA, BB, BC, CA, CB or CC give a solution. Again since none of these do, we would then look at the combinations of tiles taken three at a time. (There are $3^3 = 27$ of them). Again none of these give a solution, so we look at the 3^4 combinations of tiles taken four at a time. During this iteration we come across the solution.

Our algorithm is clearly not efficient and rather slow to run. For example, if A is not a solution, then neither AA nor AAA can possibly be solutions; it would be quicker if we did not check them. However, our goal is to give a simple algorithm that is easy to describe. We are not concerned with its efficiency or how fast it runs. Our only interest is in what it does and whether it ends after a finite period of time.

Algorithm I, though time-consuming, will eventually come across a solution if it exists, so it works in every case where the catalog of tiles has a solution to the correspondence problem. On the other hand Algorithm I does not work well if we give it a catalog of tiles for which there is no solution — it just keeps running for ever.

Could there be a different algorithm that would tell us that there is no solution in the cases where the catalogs of tiles do not have a solution? The answer is no. If such an algorithm existed — call it Algorithm II, we could construct Algorithm III that says given a catalog run both Algorithm I and II simultaneously. If the catalog has a solution to the correspondence problem, then Algorithm I will tell us this after a finite amount of time. If the catalog does not have a solution, then Algorithm II will tell us this after a finite time. This means that Algorithm III is an algorithm that tells us whether or not a catalog has a solution to the correspondence problem, but Post's result shows that such an algorithm cannot exist. The consequence is that Algorithm II cannot exist.

It is worth looking a little further into what this means. As we have noted Algorithm I is rather slow and plodding, but what if we implemented it on a fast computer and gave it a long time? For instance, if the algorithm was implemented on the fastest computer in the world and we input our first catalog of tiles, then it would give us our answer practically immediately. Given any catalog, we could then input it into the computer. Could we let it run for a long time — ten years say — and if it hasn't produced a result in this time conclude that it will run for ever and consequently the catalog that we input doesn't have a solution? Again the answer is no. If the answer were yes, we would have our Algorithm II, which we know does not exist. From this argument we can infer that there must be a catalog that has a solution, but is such that the fastest computer in the world running Algorithm I will not find it in ten years.

From Post's result that there is no solution to the correspondence problem, or equivalently no algorithm that decides this decision problem, we have deduced some rather surprising facts. First, given any time interval, say a century, and any program that tries to solve the correspondence problem, there must be a catalog of tiles that has a solution, but will take the program more than the time interval to find. The second fact we can deduce is that the real problem lies with catalogs that don't have solutions. There are algorithms that can answer the decision problem correctly in the case when the answer is yes, though they sometimes take an incredibly long time, but there are no algorithms that will also give correct answers in every case when the answer is no.

The correspondence problem with more symbols

The problem we have looked at has strings of 1s and 2s. We can consider cases where where we have more than just two symbols. In these cases, since adding more symbols is not going to make things simpler, the problem of deciding whether catalogs of tiles have a solution to the correspondence problem will also be undecidable. The following is an example of a catalog where we use the symbols 0, 1, A, B and *.

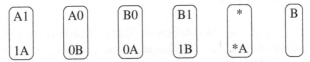

This example will tie into the next chapter. It has many solutions. It is a helpful exercise to find a few.

You could also ask what happens if we reduce the number of symbols to just one. In this case the solution is a question of whether there is a way of arranging the tiles so that the number of symbols in the top sequence is equal to the number of symbols in the bottom sequence.

Here is an example to try.

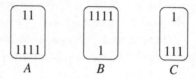

A   B   C

When we only have one symbol there is an easy way of proceeding. For each tile, we associate a number that is obtained by taking the number of symbols in the top row minus the number of symbols in the bottom row. (In the example A would be assigned -2, B assigned 3 and C assigned -2.) If there is a tile that is assigned 0, then that tile by itself is a solution. If there is at least one tile in the catalog that is positive and another that is negative, then the correspondence problem has a solution. If all the tiles are have positive numbers, or all have negative numbers, there is no solution. This gives an algorithm for deciding whether or not a catalog of tiles will, or will not, have a solution. Consequently, the correspondence problem is decidable if we restrict our tiles to just using one symbol.

In our example, we have a tile with a positive number and another with a negative number. Consequently, there must be a solution. To actually find a solution, look for a combination that totals 0. The three As are assigned a total of -6 and the two Bs assigned $+6$, so $AAABB$ is a solution.

Hilbert's Tenth Problem

In 1900, at the dawn of a new century, Hilbert listed twenty three problems that he considered the most important unanswered questions in mathematics. These questions were extremely influential in shaping the direction of mathematics research during the first half of the twentieth century. The first of the problems was Cantor's Continuum Hypothesis, which we will discuss later. The second problem was to prove that the axioms of arithmetic are consistent. As we noted, Gödel proved that it is impossible to prove the consistency of the axioms from within the system. The tenth problem concerned Diophantine equations.

A *Diophantine equation* is a polynomial equation with integer coefficients. We want to find integer solutions. A famous example is the equation

$$x^2 + y^2 = z^2,$$

which comes from the Pythagorean theorem, solutions are called *Pythagorean triples* and correspond to lengths of the sides of right triangles. Well-known Pythagorean triples are $3, 4, 5$ and $5, 12, 13$. Although there are infinitely many positive integer solutions to $x^2 + y^2 = z^2$, there are no positive integer solutions to $x^3 + y^3 = z^3$, some Diophantine equations have solutions, some do not.[2]

Hilbert's tenth problem was to devise an algorithm that would take a Diophantine equation as input and tell us whether or not it had a solution consisting of positive integers. This is a decision problem. If you input $x^2 + y^2 = z^2$, it would say yes. If you input $x^3 + y^3 = z^3$, it would say no. Again, it turns out that this is an example of an undecidable decision problem. Yuri Matiyasevich gave the completed proof in 1970. It built on the work of Martin Davis, Hilary Putnam and Julia Robinson. The proof is beyond the scope of this book, but again let us look at the consequences of what it means for this problem to be undecidable.

Consider this algorithm: First count the number of variables in the Diophantine equation. Then try plugging in 1 for each variable and see if it is a solution. If you have found a solution, stop. Otherwise, try plugging in all combinations of 1 and 2 for the variables. If you haven't found a solution, try pugging in all possible combinations of 1, 2 and 3. And so on.

If there is a positive integer solution, our algorithm will find it. For our example of $x^2 + y^2 = z^2$, we will find a solution when we have reached the iteration that consists of plugging in all possible combinations of the integers from 1 to 5. However, if we input $x^3 + y^3 = z^3$ into the algorithm, it runs forever. Since we know Hilbert's tenth problem is undecidable, and we have an algorithm that can answer the question correctly in cases when there is a solution, we can deduce that there can be no algorithm that correctly identifies Diophantine equations that don't have positive integer solutions.

The Halting Problem

We have all typed something into a computer and then seen the computer get stuck. It would be nice if there was an algorithm that told us whether or not a program would halt on a given piece of data. This is the *halting problem*. Given a program and initial data, determine whether the program will eventually halt on the data. This is another decision problem — and it is also undecidable. It also has the same property as the other two decision problems. There is an algorithm that works in the case when the answer is yes, but no algorithm in the case when the answer is no. In this case the algorithm is just to run the program on the data. If it halts, print "Yes." [3]

Back to Turing at Cambridge

Of course, all of these examples of undecidable decision problems weren't known when Turing was writing his paper. Turing and Church would be the first to understand that certain problems were undecidable. Hilbert's Entscheidungsproblem was, given a decision problem, find an algorithm that would answer the problem correctly in every case. Hilbert was making the implicit assumption that such an algorithm existed — that all decision problems were decidable. If Turing could prove that some of these problems were not decidable, then he would show that the Hilbert's approach to the Entscheidungsproblem was fundamentally flawed. He faced quite a challenge. He needed to find an undecidable decision problem that he could prove was undecidable. His proof would have to show that there was no algorithm for solving the problem. However, at this time there was no definition of what it meant to be an algorithm. The first step was to give a precise meaning to the term. This is when he invented the theoretical computing machine.

3 Finite Automata

Introduction

Automata are simple theoretical models of computing machines. In this book we will look at two types: finite automata and Turing machines.

Nowadays finite automata are thought of as stripped down Turing machines. They don't have the computational power of Turing machines, but they are able to do some non-trivial computations. They are easier to understand and to work with, and so it makes sense to study them before studying their more complicated relatives — and this is exactly what we will do in this book. However, even though they are simpler, finite automata were first introduced several years after Turing had defined his machines. They also looked quite a bit different from the way we now describe them.

Warren McCulloch was an M.D. specializing in brain injuries and working with psychiatric patients. He wanted to develop a theory of the how the brain worked. Walter Pitts was trained as a logician but had begun publishing papers in a new area that was being called *Mathematical Biophysics*. They met around 1942 and immediately recognized that they were interested in the same types of questions and that they made a good team. The expertise of one complemented that of the other.

The first paper that they published was called *A Logical Calculus of the Ideas Immanent in Nervous Activity*. In it they modeled neurons by *cells*. Each cell had a number of inputs, but only one output. The output of the cell had to terminate as the input of another cell. The inputs could be one of two types, *inhibitory* or *excitatory*. Cells fired if the number of excitatory inputs exceeded a certain threshold and there were no inhibitory inputs. This collection of cells and their connections they called a *neural net*.

McCulloch and Pitts realized that this was a simplified model of how brains actually worked, but studied neural nets to see how logic could be handled by them. Since their nets had basic features in common with neurons and the human brain, their work, they hoped, would shed some light on logical reasoning in people.

Their paper caught the attention of both John von Neumann and Norbert Wiener. Both were very impressed. Wiener, the famous American mathematician and philosopher, saw the power of feedback loops. He realized that they were widely applicable and used this idea to develop the theory of cybernetics.[1] Cybernetics naturally led to the idea of machines that could learn and, in turn, led to the birth of artificial intelligence.

Von Neumann recognized that McCulloch and Pitt's description of cells and their connections could also be applied to electrical components and computation. He described this in detail in the paper *First draft of a report on the EDVAC*, which as we will see later, is one of the most of the important papers leading to the construction of modern computers.[2]

Another person influenced by this paper was Marvin Minsky. In his Ph.D. thesis in 1954, Minsky studied neural nets, as described by McCulloch and Pitts, and showed how these fit into a comprehensive description of automata. His book, *Computation: Finite and Infinite Machines* is a classic in the field and helped usher in the modern description of automata and the theory of computation. Minsky, in the preface, describes how this theory of using theoretical machines works by comparing it to physics:

Instead of *statistically defined* events used in physics, we use *logically-defined classes* of computations or expressions. They are tied together, not by geometric or energetic properties, but by their relations to similar machines or similar definitions. We can use machine parts so simple and with such simple interactions that we can apply the utterly transparent *Logic of Propositions*, where for an equivalent actual physical machine we would have to solve hopelessly opaque analytic equations.

Automata, as Minsky's title suggests, are divided into two classes; those with finite memory and those with infinite memory. As might be suspected, it is best to start the study of them with the finite case, and this is what we shall do.

Finite Automata

A finite automaton is a simple theoretical computing machine. It consists of a finite number of *states*. There are two types of special states: The *start state*, where we start each calculation, and some *accept states*. The input to the machine consists of a sequence of symbols.

We often refer to the set of symbols as being an *alphabet* even if, as often is the case, they are the digits 0 and 1; and refer to the sequence of symbols as being a *string*. (The elements of an alphabet are often called *letters*, even if they are actually digits.)

The machine starts in the start state and reads the first symbol on the input string. There is a list of rules that tell which state the machine should move to next. Each rule is based on the state the machine is currently in and on the input symbol currently being read. After the machine has moved into its new state, the next input symbol is read, the appropriate rule is looked up, it moves to the assigned state, and the process repeats. The calculation halts when we come to the end of the input string. The initial input string is *accepted* if we end in an accept state and is *rejected* if we end in a state that is not an accept state.

The information above is more easily understood if visualized using diagrams and that is how we will introduce our various examples. In the following diagrams, the states are represented by circles. The name of the state is listed in the center of the circle. The start state is the one state that has an arrow entering it that doesn't come from another state. The accept states are denoted by double circles. The arrows connecting states are labeled by the input symbols that take us from one state to another. This is much easier to follow if we look at a specific example.

Our First Machine

In figure 1 we show our first finite automaton, M_1. The start state is labeled A — the state with the little arrow attached — and there is one accept state labeled B — the state with the double circle. The two arrows that leave A tell us that if we are in state A and a 0 is input we remain in

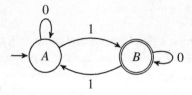

Figure 1

M_1: Strings with an odd number of 1s.

state A, and if 1 is input, we move from state A to state B. Similarly, if we are in state B and a 0 is input we stay in state B; if a 1 is input, we move to state A. The machine M_1 switches states when it sees a 1. It remains in its current state when it sees a 0.

Suppose we are given the input string 101. The machine begins in the start state A and reads the first input symbol, 1. It then moves to state B and reads the second input symbol, 0. It then remains in state B and reads the next symbol, 1. After reading this it switches back to state A. It goes to read the next symbol, but the string has ended and so the machine stops. Since we ended in state A and A is not an accept state, the string 101 is rejected by M_1.

Let us repeat the process with a different input string, 100. The machine, as always, begins in state A and reads the first input symbol which, in this case, is 1. It then moves to state B and reads the second input symbol, 0. It remains in state B and reads the next symbol, 0. It remains in B. It goes to read the next symbol, but the string has ended and so the machine stops. Since we ended in in state B and this is an accept state, the string 100 is accepted by M_1.

We can describe in words which strings M_1 will accept and which it will reject. The key point to note is that we only switch states when we see a 1. Since there are only two states, and we start in a non-accepting state, we will be in state A after an even number of 1s have been input and in state B after an odd number of 1s are input. As B is the only accept state we know that the machine accepts strings that have an odd number of 1s and rejects strings that have an even number of 1s.

This machine can be thought of as checking the parity (evenness/oddness) of the input string. Parity checking can be used as a simple way of checking for errors in transmission. We will see an example of this in the next section.

Alphabets and Languages

As we have already seen, an alphabet is just a set of symbols. Our standard Latin alphabet in use for the English language has twenty six symbols if we restrict to just the lower case. The example with the machine M_1 uses an alphabet consisting of just 0 and 1, so it is a binary alphabet. In the previous chapter we looked at tiles for the correspondence problem. In one example we were using 1 and 2 which again forms a binary alphabet. In another example we only had the one symbol 1 — a unary alphabet.

Another example of an important alphabet that was once widely used, is the one associated to Morse code. It is sometimes said that each letter in the Latin alphabet is represented by dots and dashes in Morse, but this is not quite correct. Each letter is represented by dots, dashes, and a terminal pause. When transmitting Morse code the pauses are just as essential as the dots and dashes. The alphabet for Morse is ternary — consisting of dot, dash, pause — not binary.

As we saw in the previous chapter, the example using the unary alphabet was quite simple, but things were more complicated when we used a binary alphabet. This is true in general. The ideas you can express with a unary language are very limited, but if you extend your alphabet by just one more letter so that it becomes binary you are able to express many more. However, increasing the size of the alphabet beyond size two does not increase the number of ideas you can express. This is because for any alphabet, of any size, there are ways of converting each letter into strings of binary digits. Consequently, any string that is written in any alphabet can be re-coded to a string using just a binary alphabet. Of course, if we are using an alphabet that contains many letters and convert to an alphabet using fewer letters, then the length of the converted string will be longer than the original.

The traditional alphabet in computer science is binary, but we could use any alphabet as long as it contained at least two letters. Indeed, some of the first computers didn't use binary and worked with strings written using standard decimals. (*ENIAC*, a computer that we will look at later, is an example.) Although a binary alphabet is not necessary for computer science, it is sufficient. Anything that we need to do using any alphabet can be recoded and done with binary. The main reason why we use binary is that it is very easy to implement in machines. The two letters can be represented by a switch that is either in the on or off position, or, alternatively, by the presence or absence of electrical charge.

The American Standard Code for Information Interchange (ASCII) is a way of encoding letters and control symbols using binary strings. Each character is encoded as a string of seven binary numbers. For example, A is encoded as 1000001 and a as 1100001. Since it is usual to send bytes, consisting of eight bits of information at a time, a parity check bit can be added for error detection.[3] This bit is added to the end of the string of each seven bits of data before it is sent. The parity bit, either a 1 or 0, is added so that the total number of 1s is even. When the string of eight bits is received the receiver checks to see that the parity is correct. If it isn't, the string must have become corrupted. A similar idea is used for credit card numbers. The last (on some cards it is the first) digit is called a *check digit* and is calculated from the other fifteen digits. Whenever you use a credit card the check digit is used as a check to see if the number has been entered correctly.[4]

Regular languages

The set of strings that any machine accepts is called the *language* of the machine, so the language of M_1 is the set of all finite strings of 0s and 1s with an odd number of 1s. If the machine is a finite automaton, the language is called a *regular language*, so the set of all finite strings of 0s and 1s with an odd number of 1s is our first example of a regular language.

Finite Automata and Answering Questions

Finite automata either accept or reject strings. We can often think of this as giving an answer of *yes* or *no* to a question. It is saying yes when it stops in an accept state and no if it stops in a state that is not accepting. Indeed they can often be thought of as giving answers to decision problems. The machine M_1 can be thought of as answering: *Does this string of 0s and 1s have an odd number of 1s?* (Notice that this is a decision problem — given an input string it becomes a yes/no question.)

Viewing the machine in this light we can assign meaning to the two states. State A corresponds to the machine having read strings with an even number of 1s and state B to strings with an odd number.

Finite automata can be considered as ways of systematically answering certain easy questions. In fact a good way of thinking about finite automata is to think of them as computer programs or algorithms. We will illustrate this idea with a couple of examples.

Consider the decision problem: *Does the input string end with the sequence 01?* We will outine how to construct a finite automaton for deciding this.

We begin by denoting the start state by S. If a string ends with 01, then we want to answer *Yes* — or equivalently want to stop in an accept state. We will denote this accept state by A.

As we begin to construct our machine, it is important to remember that we can only read one input symbol at a time. We are not allowed to look ahead and so we never know in advance that the input string is about to end. We discover the end of the string when we go to read an input symbol and there isn't one.

Let us consider various cases. Suppose that the first input symbol is 0. It could be that the input string is 01 which we want to accept. Seeing the initial 0 could mean that we are on our way to the accept state. We will let B denote the state that says the machine has just read a 0. If we are in state B and we see a 1, then we want to move to the accept state A. If we are in state A and we receive another input symbol, then we need to leave.

To summarize: The accept state A corresponds to having just read in 01 and state B corresponds to having just read in a 0. State S can be thought of as the start state and the state that corresponds to neither A nor B.

Once we have attached meanings to the states it is straightforward to determine the transitions between states upon reading input symbols. For example, if we are in state S and receive a 1, we want to stay there; if we receive a 0, we should move to state B. If we are in state B and we receive a 0, we should stay there; if we receive a 1, we should move to the accept state. If we are in the accept state and we receive a 0, we should move to B; if we receive a 1, we need to go all the way back to S.

The resulting finite automaton is depicted in figure 2.

Negations of questions

Interchanging the accept and non-accept states answers the negation of the question answered by the first machine. The question *Does this string of 0s and 1s not have an odd number of number of 1s* or in less convoluted form: *Does this string of 0s and 1s have an even number of 1s?* is answered by M_3 in figure 3. This is M_1 with the accept and non-accept states interchanged.

Notice that M_3 accepts 000 because we just remain in state A. This is correct because 000 contains zero 1s and zero is an even number. For the same reason, M_3 accepts 00, 0 and even the string with no symbols, the empty string, denoted by ε. In fact, it is always the case that if the start state is also an accepting state that the machine will accept ε. This is just

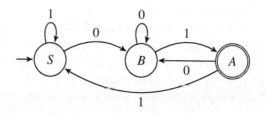

Figure 2
M_2: Strings that end with 01.

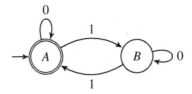

Figure 3

M_3: Strings with an even number of 1s.

saying that since the machine starts in the accept state before anything is input it will accept the empty input string that doesn't have any symbols.

The observation that interchanging the accept and non-accept states of a finite automaton answers the negation of the original question tells us that the complement of a regular language is also a regular language, that is, if we are given a regular language and then look at the collection of strings that don't belong to the language, this collection of non-belonging strings is also a regular language. This observation may seem trivial, but it is important. When we look at Turing machines we will see that sometimes the complement of a language of a Turing machine is not the language of any other Turing machine. Indeed, it is exactly this property that underlies the undecidable decision problems that we looked at earlier.

Omitting Traps from Diagrams

There are certain conventions that help simplify the pictures of our theoretical computing machines. One of the most useful is to omit non-accepting traps. In the next chapter, where we will introduce Turing machines, every diagram will be drawn using this convention. We start with an example to illustrate how this is done.

Consider the question *Does the input string start with the sequence 01?* If we receive a 0 and then a 1, we want to accept the string, so after receiving 01 our machine must be in an accept state and must remain there no matter what symbols are received afterwards. If we receive 1 as

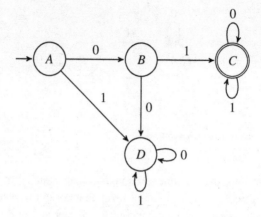

Figure 4

M_4 : Strings that start with 01.

the initial symbol we want to enter a reject state and then remain there no matter what symbols follow. An automaton that does this is shown in figure 4.

This automaton has two states that once entered it is impossible to leave. These states are called *traps*. In M_4 both C and D are traps. Often to simplify the pictures of automata, traps that are not accept states are omitted from the diagram. This is shown in figure 5, which is a diagram of the same machine as in figure 4. In figure 4 state D is a non-accepting trap. This state has been omitted from the diagram in figure 5. Notice that in figure 5 there is no arrow from A that tells us what to do if we have a 1 as input. It is assumed that if we are in A and a 1 is input that we are then forced into a trap that is not accepting, but, colloquially we say that if we are in A and a 1 is input the computation *dies*. Similarly, if the machine is in state B and receives an input of 0 the computation dies.

Of course, it is important to remember that the traps are still there even if they have been omitted from the picture. To construct the finite automaton that answers the negative question, *Is this a string that does not start with* 01, you must interchange all the accept and non-accept

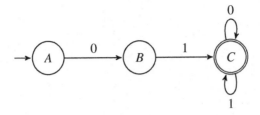

Figure 5
M_4 with state D omitted.

states. To do this, you must use the diagram given in figure 4, not the one in figure 5.

Some Basic Facts

What is the simplest finite automaton? Is there more than one way of constructing a finite automaton to answer a question? These are two basic questions that we briefly look at in this section.

The simplest finite automata

The simplest finite automata are the ones that have just one state. These are given in figures 6 and 7. The machine M_5 accepts all possible strings of 0s and 1s whereas M_6 rejects every string. (The diagram for M_6 has just one state that is not an accept state and is a trap. Our convention is that we omit non-accepting traps to help simplify the pictures, but this is the one case where omitting the state doesn't yield a helpful diagram!)

Equivalent automata

It is natural to ask is whether there is just one way of constructing a finite automaton to answer a question, or whether it is possible to have two different automata that recognize exactly the same strings. A simple construction shows that it is possible to have two very different looking finite automata that are equivalent, that is, they recognize exactly the same strings.

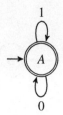

Figure 6

M_5: Accepts all strings of 0s and 1s.

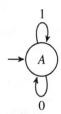

Figure 7

M_6: Doesn't accept any string.

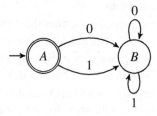

Figure 8

M_8: Accepts ε but nothing else.

Construct M_7 by taking M_1 and making every state an accepting state. Since every state of M_7 is an accept state it will accept every string. This means it is computationally equivalent to M_5. This tells us that there can be more than one way of designing a machine to answer a question. This is, of course, what we expect. There should be more than one way of answering a question.

However, for finite automata, it can be proven that there is a unique machine with the least number of states. (This can be thought of as saying that there is a unique simplest machine.) The machine M_1 has two states. It is impossible to design a machine to only accept strings with an odd number of 1s with less than two states. Consequently, M_1 is a machine with the least number of states for this question, so it is unique. If you design a different machine that answers the question it will either be M_1 or it will have more states.

We end this section with a warning. When looking to see if two machines are computationally equivalent, great care must be taken with the empty string ε. Though it is a string with zero symbols it is still a valid string. Machine M_8 helps to make this clear. It accepts ε, but no other strings. This machine is not equivalent to M_6 which doesn't accept any strings.

Now that we have seen examples of finite automata, you are probably wondering exactly how powerful these machines are. What questions can they answer? What sort of questions are beyond them? We answer these questions in the next two sections.

Regular Expressions

Stephen Kleene found an elegant way of describing the languages of finite automata — *the regular languages*.

Kleene was a student of Alonzo Church. Together they developed the λ-calculus, which Church used in his famous paper on the decision problem. Later, Kleene defined regular expressions and showed that these exactly described the languages of finite automata.

A regular expression uses whatever alphabet is used for the input tape plus additional symbols including:

The parentheses are used in the standard way to group things, but the other two symbols have special meanings. It probably should be emphasized that + does *not* mean addition and * does *not* mean multiplication.

Instead, the symbol + is used to denote a choice of the expression on the left or the right of it. So the expression $0 + 1$ stands for the two strings

0 and 1. The expression $0(0 + 1)$ stands for the two strings that begin with 0 and for which we have a choice of either 0 or 1 for the second symbol, i.e, 00 and 01. Consequently, we can write $0(0 + 1) = 00 + 01$. Similarly, $(0 + 1)(0 + 1)$ stands for the four strings of length two that begin with either 0 or 1 and end with either a 0 or 1, so

$$(0 + 1)(0 + 1) = 00 + 01 + 10 + 11.$$

We let ε denote the empty string — the string with no symbols in it. The expression $(\varepsilon + 0 + 1)(0 + 1)$ stands for the strings that start with ε, 0 or 1 and end with either a 0 or 1. (Note that $\varepsilon 0$ means exactly the same thing as 0, which gives $\varepsilon 0 = 0$. Similarly, $\varepsilon 1 = 1$.) So we have:

$$(\varepsilon + 0 + 1)(0 + 1) = \varepsilon 0 + \varepsilon 1 + 00 + 01 + 10 + 11$$
$$= 0 + 1 + 00 + 01 + 10 + 11.$$

The symbol $*$ is called the *star* or *Kleene star* operation. This operation denotes concatenating the expression with itself a finite number of times. (This also includes zero times.) The expression 0^* means any finite concatenation of 0s, that is,

$$0^* = \varepsilon + 0 + 00 + 000 + 0000 + \ldots.$$

A commonly used expression using the star operation is $(0 + 1)^*$, which is equivalent to

$$\varepsilon + (0 + 1) + (0 + 1)(0 + 1) + (0 + 1)(0 + 1)(0 + 1) + \ldots.$$

This in turn equals

$$\varepsilon + 0 + 1 + 00 + 01 + 10 + 11 + \ldots,$$

which is a list of all possible finite strings that can be formed out of 0s and 1s.

For example, if you want to list all finite strings that begin with two 1s and end with three 0s, you can write this succinctly as $11(0 + 1)^*000$.

Regular expressions describe strings of possible input symbols. A regular expression is defined to be any expression that can be formed using just these symbols.

Kleene showed that given any regular expression you can design a finite automaton to accept just the strings defined by the expression. He also showed the converse that, given any finite automaton, the strings that it accepts can be described by a regular expression. In this sense we can consider regular expressions and finite automata as equivalent. They both describe exactly the same sets of strings.

The language of M_2 is the set of all strings that end with 01. This can be described by the regular expression $(0 + 1)^*01$. The language of M_4 is the set of all strings that begin with 01. This has the regular expression $01(0 + 1)^*$. Just as there can be more than one machine for a regular language there can be more than one regular expression that describes the same language.

It should also be pointed out that some simple machines can have quite complicated regular expressions. The language of M_1 is an example. This is the language that consists of all strings that have an odd number of 1s. It is not immediately obvious how to describe this using a regular expression, but we will show how to convert the machine to an expression in a step-by-step way. Kleene's proof of the equivalence of regular expressions and finite automata has two parts. In the first part, he shows that strings represented by any finite automata can be expressed as a regular expression. In the second, he proves the converse. Our example of converting M_1 to a regular expression shows the key steps of the first part of Kleene's proof.[5]

The machine starts in state A. If a string is to be accepted, it must finish in state B. We now ask what will it have read when it first enters B. It might have gone around the 0 loop many times first, but to get to B it must then see a 1. This can be written as 0^*1. The machine is now in state B. It is possible that it might leave B at some point and then return. This would result from seeing a possible string of 0s, staying in B, and then a 1 to take us back to A. These strings would also have the form 0^*1. As before, strings from A back to B can be represented by 0^*1. This means that if the machine leaves B and returns, it must have seen the string 0^*10^*1. Of course, it is possible for the machine to never leave B again, or even to leave B many times. This can all be represented by the expression $(0^*10^*1)^*$. After the last time the machine switches states from A to B, it might remain in B for some time. This corresponds to the machine was reading a string of 0s. This can be represented by 0^*. Putting everything together gives us the expression $0^*1(0^*10^*1)^*0^*$ as the regular expression that gives the language of M_1.

Kleene's result tells us what finite automata can do. They recognize strings that are defined by regular expressions. This is often used in word and text processors. For example, if we had a document that had parts written with American spelling and parts with English spelling and we wanted to find and replace the word *color* or *colour* with *red*, we could search for the string $colo(\varepsilon + u)r$. We enter the search string using a regular expression, then to find the string, the computer simulates a corresponding finite automaton.

Regular expressions describe patterns. Tools that use these expressions form part of almost every modern programming language. Learning how to use these is an important practical skill.[6]

We now have two ways for working with finite automata, by either constructing a finite automaton or constructing a regular expression that describes the associated language. Though, in theory, any question about finite automata can be answered by using either tool, in practice, one often seems easier use than the other. We saw that with the language for M_1 it was straightforward to find the automaton, but the regular expression was quite complicated. For other examples, consider the two questions: *Can you design a finite automaton to accept stings that begin with* 000 *and end with* 111? and *Is the complement of a regular language a regular language?*

The first question is easily answered in the affirmative by constructing the regular expression $000(0 + 1)^*111$. This expression clearly describes the language. Designing an automaton for this language seems harder and less intuitive.

We have already answered the second question by looking at machines and interchanging accept and non-accept states. This is an example where considering automata makes it easy to see the answer. Using regular expressions to answer the question seems quite a bit more difficult.

We will return to this observation when we look at the definitions of *algorithm*. We will have several definitions that are equivalent. Each definition gives a different viewpoint and each one gives a different way of understanding and thinking about what computation really means, some questions that seem opaque from one vantage point become crystal clear when viewed from another.

Limitations of Finite Automata

We now turn to the question of what problems are too difficult for finite automata. We want to construct problems that we can convincingly *prove* are beyond their abilities to solve. It is not enough to construct some complicated problems that we feel are beyond their capabilities. We want proofs. To devise these proofs, we need to know what are the limiting factors of finite automata.

The major limitation comes from the fact that the only way of storing a new bit of information is by entering a new state. Finite automata only have a finite number of states, and so they can only remember a finite number things. The maximum number of different pieces of information a machine can distinguish is equal to the number of states the machine has. For example, machine M_1 only needs two states because we only need two pieces of information — whether the number of 0s is even or odd.

Given a particular finite automaton we know that it has a fixed number of states — this number could be very large, but it must be finite — let us denote it by s. Consequently the automaton will be able to distinguish s pieces of information at most. However large s is, it is easy to construct examples that will need more than s pieces of information to solve. We give two such examples below. But first we present the *pigeonhole principle*[7] that we need to use in the subsequent proofs.

The pigeonhole principle concerns putting objects into containers. It makes the obvious, but useful, observation that if there are more objects than containers, then one of the containers must contain more than one object.

Same number of 0s and 1s

The question is: *Given a string of 0s and 1s, does the number of 1s equal the number of 0s?*

This is an example of a question that is beyond the ability of finite automata to answer. To see why, let us first consider the case of whether there is an automaton with five states that could answer the question. We will show that the answer is *no* by showing that however we construct a five-state automaton, we are always able to construct two input strings — one with an equal number of 0s and 1s and the other with an unequal number — that our five-state automaton cannot distinguish.

Suppose we have a five-state automaton. Consider six input strings: 0, 00, 000, 0000, 00000 and 000000. We are performing six runs of our machine. We look to see which of the five states of the machine is the final state in each of these six runs. The pigeonhole principle tells us that at least two of the runs must end in the same state. Suppose, for example, that 00 and 00000 end in the same state after being input into the machine. If this is the case, then the two new strings 0011 and 0000011 must end in the same final state. We now have a problem. The machine either accepts both 0011 and 0000011 or it rejects both of them depending on whether or not this final state is an accept state. If our machine was able to answer the question *Given a string of 0s and 1s, does the number of 1s equal the number of 0s?*, it should accept 0011 and reject 0000011, but it doesn't.

Though I have presented this argument with specific cases, it is straightforward to generalize to any automaton with any number of states: Given any finite automaton, start feeding it $0, 00, 000, \ldots$. Identify two of these strings that end in the same state. (The pigeonhole principle guarantees that this will happen once the number of strings exceeds the number of states.) These two strings will have different lengths. Add on the same number of 1s to both strings in such a way that one of the new strings has an equal number of 0s and 1s. It is then clear that the other string will have an unequal number 0s and 1s and the machine cannot distinguish between the two strings.

Balanced brackets

Word processors often have a built in feature that determines whether the parentheses in an expression are properly balanced. For example, $((()())())$ is balanced but $())(()$ is not. To have balanced brackets, it is not enough to just have the same number of left and right brackets but they must be paired in the correct way with the left bracket to the left of its corresponding right bracket. The balanced bracket question is: *Given a string of (s and)s, are they properly balanced?*

Though this is a different problem from the previous one considering number of 0s and 1s, we can use exactly the same idea as the one above to show that the problem is too difficult for a finite automaton to solve. Instead of initially inputting strings of 0s, input strings of (s. The rest of the argument should be clear.

These two problems, though beyond finite automata, both have simple algorithms for solving them. We will give some in the next chapter. It will be a helpful exercise for the reader to think about how to construct step by step methods for answering these questions. Given a string of brackets, how do you tell if they are balanced?[8]

Tapes and Configurations

If we were to actually build a concrete example of a finite automaton, the machine could read the input in various ways. For example it might be done using a bluetooth connection or over Wi-Fi, but we are not building physical machine so we are free to choose an input mechanism that is simple to visualize and easy to work with. Turing introduced the paper tape input and that is what we will use.

Consider a computation done on M_1, the first automaton that we considered in this chapter.

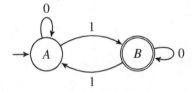

As before we will input 100. We will imagine that this string is written on a tape and that M_1 has a tape head that can read symbols from the tape. The head moves along the tape one cell at a time from left to right. In pictures we will label the head with the current state of the machine.

The following depicts the first three steps, before the machine halts at the end of the input:

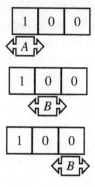

The same information can be given without drawing the tape and head. Instead of showing the state directly below the symbol being read we list it to the right. The computation can be given as $A100$, $1B00$, $10B0$, $100B$. Each of the strings tells what is written on the tape, where the head is located (or equivalently which symbol will be read next) and the current state of the machine. These strings are called *configurations*.

We list the computation in terms of the configurations again. This time one configuration above the next. This form will help to see the connection to the correspondence problem.

$$A100$$
$$1B00$$
$$10B0$$
$$100B$$

Connection to the Correspondence Problem

We will explain the connection to Post's correspondence problem by continuing to look at machine M_1. If we are in state A and and a 0 is input then we stay in state A. This means that if we have . . . $A0$ . . . as the configuration at one point in the calculation, the next configuration will be . . . $0A$ . . . . More concisely, we can say that $A0$ must be followed by $0A$.

Similarly $A1$ is followed by $1B$, $B0$ is followed by $0B$, and $B1$ is followed by $1A$. This information can be written in the form of tiles:

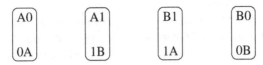

There are now a couple of tricks. The first is the introduction of the tile with $*$ on the top row and $*A$ on the bottom row. This forces us to begin with this tile and this makes us start with the correct beginning state, namely the start state A. We also need a tile for the accept state. This is done with a tile that has B on the top and a blank underneath. The complete collection of tiles is:

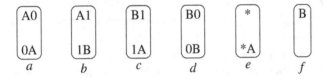

We will now find a solution to the correspondence problem. Recall that we want a line of these tiles, possibly with repetitions, such that the top sequence of symbols is equal to the bottom sequence.

We are forced to start with tile e, the only tile with initial symbols that agree. We can then use either tiles a or b. We will find the solution to the correspondence problem that corresponds to inputting 100, so we choose tile b. We have three choices for tiles we can put down next, c, d or f. The one that corresponds to our calculation is d, but note that f would also solve the correspondence problem (this corresponds to the string 10). Again we have three choices for tiles we can put down next, c, d or f. We choose d once more. As before we can then put down c, d or f, but we choose f this time to give a solution.

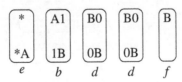

The first tile was used to force us to start in state A. Each of the other tiles corresponds to the calculation given by configurations at the end of the previous section.

Given any string of 0s and 1s that machine M_1 accepts, there is an equivalent solution of the correspondence problem using our collection of tiles. Conversely, any solution to the correspondence problem gives a string of 0s and 1s that M_1 accepts.

This idea of converting a finite automaton to a correspondence problem by using tiles that correspond to configurations works in every case. Indeed, the same idea can be applied to Turing machines. Once we see that any algorithm can be given by Turing machine, we will see that any algorithm can be described by a correspondence problem.

Finite automata are very simple machines and they are completely understood. There are no undecidable questions concerning these machines. There are algorithms for determining whether two automata are equivalent and the correspondence problem that comes from catalogs of tiles from automata is decidable.

Though these machines are very restricted in what they can do, they don't need to be modified much to turn them into powerful computing machines. This is what we do in the next chapter where we allow the machine to write on the tape. This seemingly small change gives rise to an immense change in computational power.

4   Turing Machines

We now return to Turing at Cambridge in 1935. He wanted to prove
Hilbert wrong by constructing a decision problem that was beyond the
capability of any algorithm to answer correctly in every case. Since there
was no definition of what it meant for a procedure to be an algorithm, his
first step was to define this clearly.

At this time the word *computer* referred to people who did computations. Turing's approach was to look at how human computers went
about their calculations and then to construct a theoretical machine that
could perform exactly the same operations. As Turing said in his 1936
paper:

Computing is normally done by writing certain symbols on paper. We may suppose this paper is divided into squares like a child's arithmetic book. In elementary arithmetic the two-dimensional character of the paper is sometimes used.
But such a use is always avoidable, and I think that it will be agreed that the two-
dimensional character of paper is no essential of computation. I assume then that
the computation is carried out on one-dimensional paper, i.e. on a tape divided
into squares. I shall also suppose that the number of symbols which may be
printed is finite.

. . . .

The behaviour of the computer at any moment is determined by the symbols
which he is observing and his "state of mind" at that moment.

. . . .

Let us imagine the operations performed by the computer to be split up into
"simple operations" which are so elementary that it is not easy to imagine them
further divided. Every such operation consists of some change of the physical

system consisting of the computer and his tape. We know the state of the system if we know the sequence of symbols on the tape, which of these are observed by the computer (possibly with a special order), and the state of mind of the computer. We may suppose that in a simple operation not more than one symbol is altered.

We will take Turing's approach and begin by analyzing how a human goes about a computation. Consider the following addition problem.

$$3745$$
$$+ \quad 237$$

Given a problem of this type we first recognize from the + sign and the layout that this is an addition problem. We will take this for granted and carefully look at how we proceed to do the calculation. We know that we begin with the rightmost column, but if we are going to spell out every detail we need to explain how we go about locating this. We scan through the columns, going from left to right, the rightmost column is the last column we read in before we see a column of blanks.

We usually don't even think about the blank symbols, but they are important to the calculation. Columns of blanks tell us where to begin, and where to end. Since they are important, it useful to have a symbol to explicitly denote them. We will use the Greek letter β (beta). Our problem can then be rewritten as:

$$\beta\,3745\beta$$
$$+ \quad \beta\,\beta 237\beta$$

Once we have located where to begin, we add up the digits in that column. There are two possible cases; the digits sum to less than ten, in which case the carryover number for the next column is zero; or the digits sum to ten or more, in which case the carryover number for the next column is one. In both cases we write down the units number and then move to the next column on the left. (In our example we begin by adding $5 + 7$ to get a carryover number of 1 and 2 as the unit.) We repeat the process, adding the digits in the column plus the carryover number; writing down the units and calculating the new carryover number. Along the way we may come across a column contains a blank and a non-blank symbol (in our example, we have a column that contains 3 and β). We need to know that in these cases β is acting like 0 and that $3 + \beta = 3$.

At each stage we move one column to the left until we come to a column consisting entirely of blanks. If there is a carryover one from the previous column we write down 1 and stop. If the carryover is zero, we don't write down anything else; we just stop.

This example illustrates what we need to do to in order to calculate. We need to read in data; we need to be able to write; and the calculation needs to be able to be broken into a finite number of simple components. These components or stages are what Turing refers to as *states of mind*, which later became abbreviated to just *states*.

A human computer has to be given data as input. Normally these are written on a page or pages of paper, but as Turing argues these could equally well be written on a tape. There is nothing essentially two-dimensional about a list of data or instructions. Also there is also no logical reason that necessitates reading more than one symbol at a time. Consequently, to invent a machine which could become a computer, it would be sufficient to have the input be on tape and be read by a tape head that could only read one symbol at a time.

He then argues that the computer needs to be able to write down the answer and intermediate calculations. Again there is no reason that this could not be done on a tape by a tape head that only writes one symbol at a time.

Finally, he argues that during the computation the computer will be in various states of mind. What the computer does next depends only on her state of mind and what she is reading from the tape.

In this way he went through how a person performs computations and showed that every operation could be done on his machines. In essence, Turing broke computations down to their elemental parts and then showed that Turing machines could perform each of these parts.

Turing was designing a theoretical machine that he was going to use to prove results about computation — he was not designing a practical machine. He wanted the machine to be as simple as possible and so he chose to have a single tape and a single tape head that could both read and write, rather than separate tapes for input and output.

You only need a few additional properties to turn finite automata into Turing machines. We begin our study by examining the changes that need to be made. The first big difference is in how a Turing machine is allowed to interact with the tape. In addition to the tape head moving to the right, it can also move to the left. (It might seem strange that the tape is stationary and the tape head moves, but this is the way Turing described it, and it has been universally accepted.) The second, and really important, change is that the tape head is able to write symbols onto the tape as well as being able to read them. Being able to write on the tape enables the machine to store intermediate results that will be needed later in the computation. It also gives the machine a way to output final results.

When we draw a diagram of a Turing machine we will include all of this extra information about what the tape head is doing on the arrow that goes from one state to another. For example, suppose that we are in state A and we read a 0 from the tape. For a finite automaton, we would just need to know which new state to enter. However for a Turing machine we need to not only know which state to move to, but what to write on the tape and in which direction to move the tape head. In our example, suppose that after reading 0 from the tape we move to state B, write over the 0 with an X and move the tape head one step to the left. We will indicate all of this information as in the diagram below.

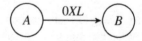

Each arrow in our diagram of a Turing machine will be labeled with three symbols; the first is the current symbol on the tape that the head is reading, the second is the new symbol that the tape head writes over the old symbol, and the third tells us whether the tape head moves left or right one step (using L for left and R for right).

Another difference between Turing machines and finite automata is that the tape is as long as we need it to be. This is often described as saying that the tape is infinite. The point is that we don't want calculations to

Chapter 4

end because the tape has run out. The tape is assumed to be long enough for any theoretical calculation. For example, if the universe contains, in total, N particles, there is no way that we can have a physical tape with $N + 1$ symbols on it, and so there is no way we can perform a calculation that needs a tape with $N + 1$ symbols written on it. However, in the theory of computation we are only interested in the theoretical limitations, not the physical ones. The fact that we cannot have $N + 1$ symbols on a physical tape tells us something about the limitations of the universe. It doesn't tell us anything about theoretical limitations of computation.

Though we say the tape is infinite, at any point in a calculation, there will be only finitely many symbols on the tape. The rest of the tape will be blank. To help indicate exactly what is on the tape it is helpful to have a symbol to denote a cell on the tape that is blank. For example, if the tape has 011 written on it, we will denote this by $\ldots \beta\beta\beta \, 011 \beta\beta\beta \ldots$, where the βs denote the infinite number of blanks on either side of our string. (This notation may seem cumbersome initially, but will be seen to be extremely useful once we look at some examples.) Often the blanks are used to let the machine know that it has reached the end of the input string — unlike finite automata that end their computations when they reach the end of their input, Turing machines can keep going. In these cases, we need some symbol to denote that the head has come to the end of the input string and is now reading a blank cell.

Another difference between Turing machines and finite automata is that Turing machines have a unique accept state and a unique reject state. Both of these states are traps. Once we reach them we can stop the calculation. If we reach the accept state during a calculation, we immediately accept the string even if not all of the input has been read. Similarly, if we reach the reject state we immediately reject the string. As in the last chapter, since the reject state is a non-accepting trap, it is standard not to depict it in the diagrams of these machines.

Lastly, the convention is that the read/write head reads the leftmost non-blank symbol of the input string when the machine starts.

Some examples of constructing and running Turing machines should help clarify all these ideas.

Examples of Turing Machines

Recognizing strings with an odd number of 1s

We start with the first example of a finite automaton from the last chapter. A machine that recognizes strings of 0s and 1s with an odd number of 1s. (This was depicted in figure 1 in the previous chapter.) As with the finite automaton we will let our Turing machine have two states, A and B, with A corresponding to the machine having seen an even number of 1s and B to having seen an odd number of 1s. For the finite automaton we could let B be an accept state. If another 1 was input, then the machine moved back to state A, indicating that an even number of 1s had now been input. We cannot do this with a Turing machine. Once a Turing machine enters the accept state it halts the computation and accepts the string. We can still let B be the state that says that we have seen an odd number of 1s, but we need a separate state to be the accept state. This third state, the accept state, we denote by C. Now we need a way to make the machine accept or reject a string after we have read the whole string. One method is to make use of the fact that after the input string has ended the tape head will see a blank. We will use this, and include an arrow from B to the accept state C when the machine sees the input symbol β.

A diagram of our Turing machine is given in figure 1. In this simple example the tape head moves to the right at each step, so the third symbol on each arrow is R. We also don't need to write anything on the tape; consequently we chose to leave the symbols as they were. This is done by rewriting the symbol with the same symbol, so each labeling of an

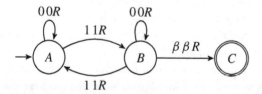

Figure 1

TM_1: Strings with an odd number of 1s.

arrow has the second symbol equal to the first. We could have erased the symbols as we read them. In this case, the middle symbol on each arrow would have been β, and the tape would then be completely blank after the computation was completed.

The final observation is that the reject state and associated arrow are omitted. If we were to include the halt state, there would be an arrow from A to the halt state labeled $\beta \beta R$.

Algorithms

In each of the following cases we will describe an algorithm for solving the problem and then construct a Turing machine to implement the algorithm. For the example that we have just considered the algorithm is: Begin with the left side of the string and move right one step at a time. At each stage keep track of whether an even or an odd number of 1s have been seen. Once we have come to the end of the input (i.e., we see a blank) accept the string if we have seen an odd number of 1s and reject the string if we have seen an even number of 1s.

Equal number of 0s and 1s

We want an algorithm for looking at a string of 0s and 1s and deciding whether there are an equal number of both. There are many ways that this can be done. You might be thinking that we could just count the number of 0s and then count the number of 1s and then see if the two numbers are equal. This is fine for humans who have mastered the art of counting, but is not the easiest way to proceed with our rather primitive machines. A far simpler way is for our Turing machine to pair a 0 with a 1 and then cross off the pair. We keep doing this until we cannot do it any more. If we have crossed off all the symbols in the string, then we know that the number of 0s must equal the number of 1s and so we accept the string. If we have a string of just 0s or just 1s left, we reject the string.

The machine will have the ability to write a new symbol, X. It will use this to write-over pairs of 0s and 1s.

We will now describe the operation of the machine in a little more detail. It is going to pair 0s and 1s. If it sees a 1 first it will replace it with an X and then look for a corresponding 0. If it finds one, it will replace the 0 with an X and return to the beginning of the input string. If it doesn't find a 0 to pair up with the 1 it halts in the reject state. In a similar way, if the machine sees a 0 first it will replace it with an X and then look for a corresponding 1.

The machine is depicted in figure 2. To understand what is going on it is helpful to attach a meaning to each of the states.

The start state S says: *I need to keep moving the head to the right looking for the leftmost 0 or 1. If I find a 0, I will replace it with an X and move to state B. If I find a 1, I will replace it with an X and move to state C. If I find an X, I leave it alone, stay in state S. If I don't find any 0s or 1s and reach a blank, I know that they must have all been paired up, and so I move to the accept state A.*

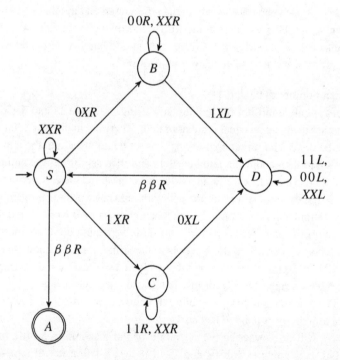

Figure 2

TM_2: Strings with an equal number of 0s and 1s.

State *B* says: *I have just seen a* 0 *and now need to find a* 1 *to pair with it. I move the head right through the tape. If I see a* 0 *or an X, then I just keep going. If I see a* 1, *then I replace it with an X and move to state D.*

State *C* is similar to state *B*, but with 0s and 1s interchanged. It says: *I have just seen a* 1 *and need to find a* 0 *to pair with it.*

State *D* is entered just after a 0-1 pair has been replaced by *X*s. The machine needs to re-set for the next count by re-winding its tape head to the left side and re-entering its start state.

State *D* says: *I have just erased a pair consisting of one* 0 *and one* 1 *and must go back to the start state. I keep moving the head leftwards through the tape ignoring everything until I see a blank, which indicates I have reached the lefthand end. I move the head right one step to get to the first non-blank symbol and go back to the start state S.*

As in the previous chapter, the reject state is not depicted because it is a trap. If you have a string with an unequal number of 0s and 1s, then you will end in either state *B* or *C* and have a β as input. This means that the machine goes to the reject state and the computation halts.

To understand this machine it helps to invent a few short strings of 0s and 1s and run them through it. A good example is the string 0011. As usual it helps to include the blank cells on either side, so our initial string is $\beta0011\beta$, and the first few steps are:

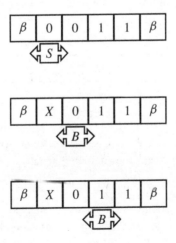

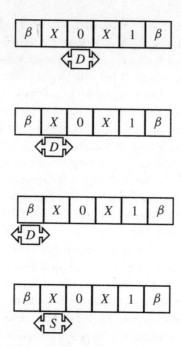

At this stage the machine has completed one iteration of canceling a pair of 0s and 1s and has returned back to the start state with the head again reading the leftmost symbol of the input string. The machine then goes through another of these iterations and, after many steps in which the remaining 0 and 1 are canceled, arrives at

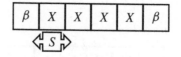

At this point the tape head keeps moving right and the machine stays in state S until it reaches the blank cell on the right. After this the machine enters the accept state and the computation halts.

Balanced brackets

The next Turing machine is for balanced brackets. As we noted at the end of the previous chapter, this is another problem that cannot be solved by a finite automaton. We will proceed as in the previous example and locate a left and right bracket and erase them by replacing them with Xs. However, pairing brackets is a little more complicated. We cannot just count the number of left brackets and the number of rights brackets and see if these two numbers are equal. We must check that the brackets are paired up correctly. For example,

$$) \quad (\quad) \quad ($$

has the same number of right and left brackets, but they are not properly balanced.

One method for determining whether the sequence is balanced is to move right along the string until you find the first right bracket. Replace it with an X. Then start moving left. The first left bracket that you come to is the partner of the bracket you have just replaced with an X, and so you replace this left bracket with an X.

The diagram of the associated Turing machine is given in figure 3. The meaning of each of the states is as follows:

State S says: *I'll keep moving the tape head to the right until I see a right bracket. When I find a right bracket I will replace it with an X and*

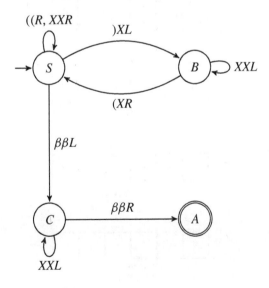

Figure 3

TM_3: Balanced brackets.

move to state B. *If I reach the end of the string without seeing a right bracket, I know that there are no right brackets remaining, and I move to state C.*

State B says: *A right bracket has just been erased, so I need to move the head leftwards through the string to find its left partner. If I find it, I replace it with an X and go back to state S. If I don't find it, I will reach a β and halt in the reject state.*

State C says: *The tape head is at the right end of the string and there are no right brackets remaining. I need to move the head to the left checking for possible left brackets. If I find one, then I halt in the reject state. If I don't, then I will eventually reach a blank cell which tells me that the entire string consists of Xs, and I go to the accept state.*

As with the previous machine, to really understand how this machine works it is extremely helpful to run it on several examples. Below are the first few steps of running the machine on the string

$$(\quad (\quad) \quad).$$

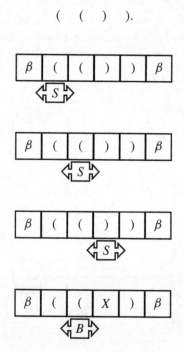

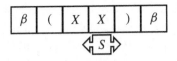

(The complete computation is in the notes.)[2]

Computable Functions and Calculations

The Turing machines we have looked at so far have been designed for answering yes/no questions. They accept strings if and only if the machine reaches the accept state. However, the machine has the ability to write on its tape and so it has another way of outputting answers. It can leave its answer on the tape. We will examine this idea briefly.

Computable functions

The natural numbers are the positive whole numbers. We will represent them in *unary* notation. This means that each number is written as 1 repeated the appropriate number of times. (For example, 4 is written as 1111.) We can look at Turing machines that start with a finite string of 1s as input and end in the accept state with a finite string of 1s on the tape. For example, we might have a machine that starts with 1111 and then ends in the accept state with 111111 on its tape. We can think of this as inputting the number 4 and getting the number 6 as output. These machines can be thought of as giving us a function from the natural numbers to themselves — we input a natural number and it outputs a natural number. These functions are called *computable functions*.

These functions play an important role in the theory of computation. Our definition is in terms of Turing machines, but other mathematicians and logicians have constructed these functions from very different starting points. In the next chapter we will look at Church's approach. The fact that these different approaches result in the same set of functions shows that they are equivalent. They are different ways of saying the same thing.

By now you probably would like to see some specific examples of functions from the natural numbers to themselves that are computable and some specific examples that are not. Suffice it to say that probably any example that you can think of will be computable. For example, functions that involve addition, multiplication, powers, and exponents will all be computable. In fact, it is quite hard to describe a non-computable function, but we will see one later, when we introduce the *busy beaver* function. (We will define this function and show why it is not computable when we analyze undecidable problems.)

Calculations

We can also design Turing machines that do standard mathematical operations. It is not too difficult to design a machine to add two natural numbers. If we want to calculate $2 + 3$, we would write this in unary and input,

$$11 + 111.$$

The machine would output,

$$11111.$$

A simple way of designing this adding machine is to erase the leading 1 (that is, overwrite it with β) and then overwrite the $+$ sign with 1.

A Turing machine for multiplying numbers can also be built. In this case, if we input

$$1111 \times 111$$

it outputs

$$111111111111.$$

We will briefly describe how the machine computes this. The first step is to erase the left most 1 and then move the tape head to the right of the $\times$ sign and replace all the 1s with Xs. At the end of this stage we would have

$$\beta 111 \times XXX.$$

The next step is to again erase the leading 1 on the left of the tape and move the tape head to the right of the $\times$ sign. This time each X is turned into a Y, but each time we turn an X into a Y we add a 1 to the right end of the string. At the end of this stage we have

$$\beta\beta 11 \times YYY111.$$

The process repeats with the left most 1 being erased; the Ys changed back to Xs with 1s being added to the end of the string; which results in

$$\beta\beta 1 \times XXX111111.$$

Repeating one more time gives:

$$\beta\beta\beta \times YYY111111111.$$

The machine now looks for the leftmost non-blank symbol. It sees $\times$. This tells it delete $\times$, change all the Ys and Xs to 1s, and then halt. This give the final answer

$$111111111111.$$

Subtraction and integer division are not much more difficult to code. Once we have machines for addition, multiplication, subtraction and division, we can combine them into one machine that does all four operations.

Church-Turing Thesis

As we noted at the start of this chapter, the first step in tackling the Entscheidungsproblem was to give a definition of an *algorithm* (or equivalently an *effective procedure*). Turing thought about what computation entails, distilled what he felt were the elemental components, and used them to give his definition of Turing machines. He then defined an algorithm to be anything that can be computed by a Turing machine.

Since this is a definition, it cannot be proved or disproved, but you can have an opinion as to whether or not the definition is appropriate. The intuitive idea of an algorithm is a step-by-step procedure for doing calculations. Turing is giving a formal definition of what it means to be a step-by-step procedure. If you agree that the definition is correct, then you are forced to accept that any algorithm whatsoever can be implemented by a Turing machine. If you don't believe that the definition is correct then you should try to come up with either a better definition or give an example of something that one intuitively feels should be called an algorithm, but cannot be carried out by a Turing machine.

Both approaches have been tried, and there is consensus that Turing has captured the essence of what it means for a procedure to be an algorithm. There are other definitions. Recall that Church's paper on the Entscheidungsproblem was published before Turing's. Church also needed to give a definition of an effective procedure. He did this via what he called the λ-calculus. As Turing read Church's paper he realized that there were now two different definitions. As he studied both definitions he realized that, though they looked very different, they were equivalent. They had both defined exactly the same concept. He then quickly added a proof of the equivalence to his paper before he submitted it for publication.

The Church-Turing thesis is that both of these definitions have captured the fundamental meaning of what it means for a process to be an algorithm. It is usually stated as follows:

Anything that can be computed can be computed by a Turing machine.

In addition to the λ-calculus, there have been other definitions of effective procedure. Post defined *canonical systems* and Kleene defined *general recursive functions*. In each case the formulations have proved equivalent to those of Church and Turing. This equivalence means that, though their approaches were different, they all describe exactly the same features or properties of what it means for a procedure to be effective.

The notation used for describing ideas in mathematics can be very important. For example, both Newton and Leibniz discovered calculus around the same time, but their notations were very different. The notation that was used by Leibniz quickly proved to be far superior to that of Newton for complicated calculations.[3] A technique of integration, called *u*-substitution, is very easy to learn using Leibniz's notation. The manipulations involved in using *u*-substitution are really an application of the chain rule, but the clever choice of notation hides this fact and makes it seem as though you are doing simple algebra.

As Bertrand Russell noted, "A good notation has a subtlety and suggestiveness which at times make it almost seem like a live teacher."[4] These comments are particularly apposite to Turing and his definition of an algorithm. Several people defined and described algorithms in very different ways, but Turing's description is remarkably easy to visualize and gives a simple framework for the study of computation. Before Church and Turing wrote their papers, Gödel wasn't sure that the idea of an algorithm could be rigorously defined. He wasn't even sure after reading Church's definition, but was immediately and thoroughly convinced by Turing's approach.

Computational Power

We have seen that Turing machines are finite automata with a few additional features. We saw that the computational power of finite automata was quite limited — the balanced bracket problem is beyond their capabilities — but that Turing machines can execute any algorithm. It is natural to wonder about adding additional features to a Turing machine. If we could add more features, could we make it even more powerful? For example, having two tapes and tape heads would be nice. We could have one tape reserved for input and one for output. While we are at it, it might be better to have a keyboard for data entry and a display for output. But no matter what additional mechanical features we add, the computational power does not increase. The new machine might be easier for us to use, but anything that it can compute can be computed by a regular Turing machine. In fact, since Turing machines are theoretical and have no limitations on the size of the input or the time needed for computation, they can do more than any real computer that is subject to limitations on the size of the input and the life of the computer.

These remarks also apply to quantum computers.[5] These computers are often described as being the next leap in computation — they will be more powerful and that they will be able to solve problems that are beyond conventional computers. The advance that quantum computing brings is speed. If practical quantum computers are constructed, they might be able to solve certain problems much faster than our current computers. In technical terms, some algorithms that take exponential time on a conventional computer could take only polynomial time on a quantum computer. We will briefly explain a little about what this means before returning to our study of computability.

Polynomial time

By time, we mean the number of steps in the calculation. We can imagine each step taking one second to perform. In general, the number of steps will depend on the size of the input string n. For each positive number n, there will be many input strings that have length n. The machine might need to take more steps for some of these strings than others, but we can ask what is the maximum number of steps required for each n. This gives a function from n, the size of the input string, to $f(n)$, the maximum number of steps to complete the computation. We then ask whether there is a polynomial in $p(n)$ such that $p(n) \geq f(n)$ for all positive integers n. If there is a bounding polynomial, then we say the algorithm is a *polynomial time algorithm*.

For an example, consider our algorithm for balanced brackets. Suppose we have an input string of length n. What is the maximum number of steps that the machine needs to determine whether the string is balanced? Recall that we need to use the blank cells on either side of the string, and that the tape head keeps moving left and right along the tape — it never stops. Once the tape head starts moving right it keeps on going right until it replaces a bracket with an X or the computation ends. Similarly, once the tape head starts moving left it keeps on going left until it replaces a bracket with an X or the computation ends. The total number of trips to the left added to the number of trips to the right must be less than or equal to $n + 1$. It equals $n + 1$ in when the string is balanced and it has to replace all n brackets with Xs. (The extra trip comes from checking that the string consists entirely of Xs.) As the tape head moves left and right, it reads the non-blank symbols on the tape and possibly the one blank cell on either side of the string. Consequently, the number of steps left or right at each stage can be at most $n + 2$, so the total number of steps in the computation must be less than or equal

$$(n + 1)(n + 2) = n^2 + 3n + 2.$$

Since the time taken for our algorithm to answer the question for an input string of length n is bounded above by the polynomial $p(n) = n^2 + 3n + 2$, we have shown that our algorithm is a polynomial time algorithm.

We can now start to classify decision problems. Decision problems that can be solved in polynomial time by Turing machines are denoted by *P*. We have shown that the problem *Is this string of brackets balanced?* belongs to *P*.

Non-deterministic Turing machines

There is a variation of the Turing machine, called a non-deterministic Turing machine, that can be in more than one state at a time and so can do several computations in parallel.

When we first introduced the Turing machine we had the following diagram which meant that when the machine was in state *A* and read 0 on the input tape, it moved to state *B*, replaced the input symbol with an *X* and then moved the tape head left.

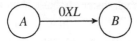

A non-deterministic Turing machine can have more than one choice for what to do when it reads an input symbol. For example, we might have a diagram such as the following.

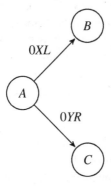

This means that when the machine is in state *A* and reads 0 on the input tape there are two choices: it moves to state *B*, replaces the input symbol with an *X* and then moves the tape head left; or it it moves to state *C*, replaces the input symbol with an *Y* and then moves the tape head right. We have to keep track of both possible choices (or branches) of the computation. At each stage there can be many choices, so there will often be many branches of the computation. If one of the branches reaches the accept state, the machine halts and the input string is accepted.

It should be stressed that, despite the name, non-deterministic Turing machines are completely determined. When describing these machines words like "choosing" or "guessing" are often used. These can be very misleading to the newcomer. It is completely determined whether or not the machine accepts its input string. Of course, to demonstrate that an input sting is accepted we just need to find a particular branch that leads to the accept state. It is in describing a particular branch that you have to give the appropriate option at each stage, and it is here where we often say that the machine is 'choosing' or 'guessing' the correct option.

Non-deterministic Turing machines calculate the branches of the computation in parallel, so they are generally faster than Turing machines, but the question is, how much faster? Is there a problem that can be solved by a non-deterministic Turing machine in polynomial time that cannot be solved in polynomial time by a regular deterministic Turing machine?

The decision problems that non-deterministic Turing machines can solve in polynomial time are denoted by NP. It is clear that P is a subset of NP, but it is still an open question of whether there are any problems that belong to NP, but not to P. In fact, there is a million dollar prize offered by Clay Mathematics Institute for the first person to give a proof of whether or not P is the same set as NP, some people conjecture that the set of problems that quantum computers can solve in polynomial time contains all of P and also some problems not in P, but not all of NP. But this is a conjecture. The proof would have to show that P is not equal to NP.

This area of the theory of computation dealing with the amount of time and storage needed to do computations based on the size of the input is known as *complexity theory*. These questions are not just of theoretical interest, but have important practical applications. Much of internet commerce requires secure ways of encrypting information. However, many of the current methods of encryption are based on methods that are conjectured, but not proven, to be exponentially difficult to crack. It would be nice to have a proof that our internet banking is safe!

Quantum computers and non-deterministic Turing machines may be faster in certain instances, but they are not computationally more powerful than Turing machines. In this book, we are looking to see which problems can be solved by computers and which cannot. To answer this, it is enough to restrict our attention to just basic Turing machines, and this is what we will do from now on.

Machines That Don't Halt

The examples of Turing machines that we have looked at so far always halt. Given any input string they either accept it by entering the accept state, or reject it by entering the reject state. However there is another possibility. It is possible to construct a machine that keeps going forever and never halts.

Consider the machine TM_4 depicted in figure 4. If the input string begins with a 0, then the machine moves to the accept state and the computation halts. If 10 is input, the machine first reads 1 and moves

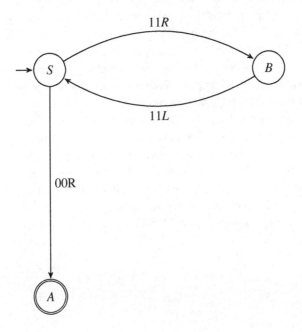

Figure 4
TM_4: Never halts on 11.

to state B. It then reads 0 and the computation dies, which means that it halts in the reject state. However, if we input 11, the machine first goes to state B and then it reads the second 1. It then moves back to state A, the tape head moves left and we are back to where we started. The process repeats forever. The computation never ends.

Consequently there are three possibilities for computations with Turing machines: A computation can halt in the accept state, it can halt in the reject state, or the computation never halts. If a computation never halts we will say that it *diverges*.

Notice that this is very different from finite automata. A finite automaton has a finite input string, the string is read from left to right and the machine halts when it gets to the end of the string. Consequently, finite automata always halt. The number of steps in the computation is exactly equal to the length of the input.

At this stage it is not clear that computations that diverge are important. One might suspect that machines that don't halt are poorly designed, and that if they were designed better they could be made to halt on every input. However, this is not the case. The fact that some computations do not halt is not a design flaw. It is not something that we can eliminate. We will see that this property that some machines diverge has important consequences for what we can compute and cannot compute.

Before we continue with our discussion of Turing machines we will take a brief detour. We noted that several different people gave very different definitions of algorithms and computation. Although Turing's definition has an elegant simplicity, the other definitions, though equivalent, give us different vantage points from which to view computation. As we commented before, things that are difficult to see from one viewpoint become easier from another. We will look at some of these ideas in the next chapter.

5   Other Systems for Computation

"We may say most aptly, that the Analytical Engine weaves
algebraical patterns just as the Jacquard-loom weaves
flowers and leaves."
Ada Lovelace

In 1823, with substantial funding from the British government, Charles
Babbage began the construction of his first "Difference Engine." The
mathematical tables of the time contained many errors that were caused
by human computers. Babbage's Difference Engine was to be a mechanical calculator. It would provide a quicker, cheaper, and more accurate
way of generating these tables. Babbage drew the plans for the machine,
but employed an engineer, Joseph Clement, to actually build it. The construction required meticulous work and proceeded slowly. Over time ten-
sions grew between Babbage and Clement. These reached a climax in
1831 when they realized that they could no longer work together and the
project was abandoned.

Though the physical machines were not constructed during his life-
time, Babbage went on to design a new difference engine, Difference
Engine No. 2, and the Analytical Engine.[1] The Analytical Engine was
far more sophisticated than the difference engines. Its most important
and innovative feature was that it could be programmed using punched
cards. This was an idea that he borrowed from mechanical looms. In
1801, Joseph-Marie Jacquard had designed a mechanical loom that could
weave intricate patterns based on operations controlled by a sequence
of punched cards. Babbage realized he could use the same idea for his
machine. He had designed the programmable computer.

Augusta Ada King, Countess of Lovelace, now usually known as just
Ada Lovelace, was the daughter of the poet Lord Byron. Her mother,
concerned about the mental instability in Lord Byron's family, decided
that her daughter should study mathematics to help build her mental
defenses. This, along with the fact that she had a natural talent for

mathematics, resulted in Lovelace being tutored and mentored by some of the best mathematicians of the time. It was natural that she and Babbage would meet.

Lovelace was intrigued by Babbage's machines. She not only understood what Babbage was trying to do, but saw the immense potential of computers. She was not the only one impressed by Babbage. In Italy, the mathematician Luigi Menabrea was also fascinated by Babbage's Analytical Engine. He wrote an article about it based on his notes from lectures that Babbage had given in Turin. Lovelace was persuaded to translate this paper into English and to add her own annotations. Instead of a few comments, she added an extensive addition to Menabrea's work — her pages of notes exceeding double the length of the original article.[2] In these notes she outlined her vision for the future of computing.

The notes are famous for including the first published computer programs, for her foresight in seeing that computers would have wide application beyond mathematics, and for what is taken as a rejection of artificial intelligence. The largest computer program was for computing Bernoulli numbers. These numbers occur in a number of areas of mathematics. To this day, there are still papers being published about how to compute these numbers efficiently. This program was written as a collaboration between Babbage and Lovelace. There is some controversy over which of them contributed the essential ideas and who really deserves the credit; nevertheless, Lovelace is often credited as being the first computer programmer.

She also realized that computers could be useful in a variety of areas. One she considered was music. There are rules for harmony and methods of music composition. Lovelace conjectured that computers might be programmed with these rules and be able to "compose elaborate and scientific pieces of music of any degree of complexity or extent."

It was also in this paper that she wrote: "The Analytical Engine has no pretensions whatever to *originate* anything. It can do whatever *we know how to order it* to perform. It can *follow* analysis; but it has no power of *anticipating* any analytical relations or truths." This is clearly a statement about what we now call artificial intelligence. Many, including Turing, think that she was wrong, but the amazing thing is that she was even considering the link between computers and brains a century before the first computer had even been built. As David Deutsch points out,[3] the error that Lovelace made was really not in underestimating computers, but in overestimating the human brain at a time when many supernatural beliefs were commonly held.

Her quote at the start of the chapter seems exactly right. Computations done on Turing machines take an input string and perform a sequence of manipulations on it. One symbol is changed at a time. Computations correspond to a sequence of changes on strings, starting with the initial input string. However, there are many ways of designing systems that "weave algebraical patterns" from an input string, and some of these systems of manipulating symbols can be thought of as computations if we interpret things correctly.

Before we continue with the study of Turing machines we will look at other ways of manipulating strings. First we look at Church's λ-calculus (lambda calculus), then Post's tag systems, and finally cellular automata. All of these have been shown to be able to do computations. In fact, rather surprisingly, all have computational power equivalent to Turing machines.

We start with the λ-calculus. This plays an important role in computer science, especially in the design of computer languages. After our brief foray into λ-calculus we move on to tag systems.

Tag systems are easy to describe, but despite their simplicity, they are able to do any computation. Their simplicity is often useful in proving the equivalence of computational systems. For example, the proof that cellular automata can do anything that Turing machines can do involves emulating Turing machines by tag systems.

The final topic is the study one-dimensional cellular automata. These are interesting because they yield two-dimensional pictures that show the entire computation. From these pictures it is possible to make conjectures about the computational power of the underlying rules.

Each of these three topics is independent of the others, and so they can be read in any order.

Though this book is about a paper written in 1936, the examples that we consider using tag systems and one-dimensional cellular automata were developed quite recently. In writing a book of this type it is very easy to give the impression that everything has been done and there is nothing new left to do. Of course, Turing's main result says exactly the opposite, that work in theoretical computer science will never be completed, so it is good to see some contemporary results that are also quite accessible.

The Lambda Calculus

The λ-calculus was developed by Church at the same time that Gödel was developing his theory of recursive functions. Kleene showed that these two theories were equivalent. Church believed that the λ-calculus described all computable functions. As a consequence, if Church was correct, Gödel's recursive functions would also describe all computable functions. Gödel was far from convinced that he and Church were describing everything that could be computed. Then, as part of his paper on the Entscheidungsproblem, Turing showed that his theory of Turing machines was equivalent to λ-calculus. Everyone was convinced that Turing had captured the essence of computation, and so Gödel realized that Church had, in fact, been correct.

Consequently, in 1937 there were three different but equivalent ways of describing computation. In the years that followed, mathematicians mainly adopted the recursive function theory approach and computer scientists adopted Turing's approach. Church's λ-calculus did not initially receive much of a following.

Church was a logician. He was very precise and careful. He expected his students to approach logic in the same way. He was extremely influential, one of the most important logicians of the twentieth century, with many of his Ph.D. students going on to have distinguished careers in logic and computer science.

The λ-calculus built mathematics carefully from the ground up — everything being defined from functions. Outsiders found this approach difficult. Even Kleene, who had helped develop the λ-calculus, eventually stopped using it. He explained that if he gave a talk using the λ-calculus hardly anyone would attend it, but if he described exactly the same ideas using recursive functions his talks would attract a crowd.

However, despite the initial unpopularity, the λ-calculus played, and is still playing, an important role in computer science.

As attested by Andrew Appel, the Eugene Higgins Professor of Computer Science at Princeton University, the λ-calculus underlies many of the ideas of current programming languages.[4] In 1958, Algol was first developed with ideas from the λ-calculus, and Lisp was developed explicitly using the λ-calculus. Most modern programming languages have evolved from these two. As Appel says, "Notions and mechanisms of variable binding, scope, functions, parameter passing, expressions, and type checking are all imported directly from Church's λ-calculus."

Before we plunge in, it will help to look at how arithmetic was formalized in the nineteenth century.

Peano arithmetic

In the first chapter we described how there were attempts to construct all of mathematics from systems of axioms. But before there were grand schemes to axiomatize everything, axiom systems were developed for various areas of mathematics. One of these areas was arithmetic. How do you define the natural numbers? How do you define addition? These were questions being asked in the nineteenth century. We will look at a succinct and powerful approach. It began with Hermann Grassmann who published his ideas in 1861. However, they did not attract much attention.[5] This approach was rediscovered by Charles Sanders Peirce and Richard Dedekind, and then polished by Giuseppe Peano into what are now known as the *Peano axioms*.

A fundamental idea is the *successor function* which we will denote by S. Once you have defined 0 and the successor function S, you can define 1 to be the successor of 0, that is, $S(0)$. Then you can define 2 by

$$2 = S(1) = S(S(0)).$$

In this way, all of the natural numbers are built up in a step-by-step process. Each number is defined from the previous one, so for example, once you have defined $0, 1, 2, 3, 4$, you can then define 5, by $5 = S(4)$. In defining 4 you observe that $4 = S(S(S(S(0))))$, and so obtain that $5 = S(S(S(S(S(0)))))$.

In every case, n turns out to be S applied n times to 0. (It is tempting to think that we could simplify things and just use this as the definition, but we cannot. It would be circular, defining n in terms of n.)

Once you have the natural numbers, you can then define addition recursively.

We define $+$ by the two properties:

$$m + 0 = m \text{ for all } m \in \mathbb{N},$$
$$m + S(n) = S(m + n) \text{ for all } m, n \in \mathbb{N}.$$

To illustrate how this defines addition, we will carefully calculate $3 + 2$ using this definition. We start by observing that $2 = S(1)$, so

$$3 + 2 = 3 + S(1).$$

The second property of the definition tells us that

$$3 + S(1) = S(3 + 1).$$

We also know that $1 = S(0)$, so

$$S(3 + 1) = S(3 + S(0)).$$

We use the second property once more to obtain

$$3 + S(0) = S(3 + 0).$$

So we have

$$3 + 2 = 3 + S(1) = S(3 + 1) = S(3 + S(0)) = S(S(3 + 0)).$$

Now we can apply the first property to deduce $3 + 0 = 3$, and so we arrive at

$$3 + 2 = S(S(3)).$$

Finally, we use that facts $4 = S(3)$ and $5 = S(4) = S(S(3))$, to reach the conclusion that

$$3 + 2 = 5.$$

The lambda calculus and functions

Church along with his students, Kleene and John Barkley Rosser, developed the λ-calculus to describe computations. The basic objects they considered were functions and the basic construction involved the idea of function composition via substitution. Functions are a sensible choice for describing computation. A function takes an input and gives an output. A computation will take the output of one function and use it as the input for another. This is exactly what we mean by *function composition* via *substitution*. We will look at a few examples to get an idea of this approach. First, we will describe the role of the symbol λ.[6]

The function that sends every point to itself, the identity function, is usually written as $f(x) = x$. This is described in the λ-calculus by $\lambda x.x$. The x on the right side of the dot plays exactly the same role as the x on the right side of the equation. The λx tells us that we are allowed to substitute for x. This is the same as saying that x is an *independent variable* or *bound variable*. The letters or names attached to bound variables have no meaning. Just as the identity function can be given as $f(x) = x$, $g(u) = u$ or $h(z) = z$; $\lambda x.x$, $\lambda u.u$ and $\lambda z.z$ all say exactly the same thing, sometimes we will change the name of a bound variable to avoid confusion. For example, we will write $(\lambda x.x)(\lambda y.y)$ instead of writing $(\lambda x.x)(\lambda x.x)$.

If we had $\lambda xz.xyz$, we would be allowed to substitute for x and z, but not for y. The bound variables are x and z. The variable y is called a *free* variable. The objects being substituted are shown on the right side of the expression, so $(\lambda xz.xyz)a$ means that one of the independent variables is replaced with a. The rule is to begin with the leftmost bound variable and move right, so $(\lambda xz.xyz)a$ becomes $\lambda z.ayz$, $(\lambda xz.xyz)ab$ becomes ayb and $(\lambda xz.xyz)(ab)$ becomes $\lambda z.(ab)yz$.

This straightforward way of substituting one expression into another forms the basis of the λ-calculus. It might look rather simplistic, but Church, Kleene, and Rosser found that they could build the natural numbers and then construct a large class of functions — the computable functions. We briefly look at how some arithmetic and logic is tackled.

These sections may seem difficult and won't be needed later. They can be omitted on first reading the book. The main difficulty comes from the unusual way of considering everything as being built from functions.

We are not used to thinking of numbers as being functions; we are not used to thinking of *True* and *False* as functions. However, performing calculations using the λ-calculus is fairly straightforward. You are always replacing symbols with other symbols according to very simple rules. Though these ideas won't be needed later, I urge the reader to at least sample them.

Arithmetic

The λ-calculus borrows some of the basic ideas about arithmetic from Peano. As with the Peano axioms we will have 0 and the successor function S. We will then define $1 \equiv S(0)$, $2 \equiv S(1) = S(S(0))$, and so on. The differences are that we give definitions for both 0 and S. These are:

$$0 \equiv \lambda sx.x,$$

$$S \equiv \lambda abc.b(abc).$$

Let us describe these two definitions in words. First, 0 is defined as the function that has two input expressions s and x. It ignores what is input for s and outputs whatever is input for x. The successor function has three input expressions or functions. It first concatenates the three functions and then substitutes this concatenation into the second input expression. There is no question that this all seems very strange when you first see it, but once you get over the initial weirdness and start working with the definitions it becomes quite simple.

We will explicitly compute a couple of numbers to show what is going on. We will begin by calculating $S(0)$ which is defined to be 1. Substituting for both S and 0 gives

$$S(0) = (\lambda abc.b(abc))(\lambda sx.x).$$

Now substituting $(\lambda sx.x)$ for a gives

$$\lambda bc.b((\lambda sx.x)bc).$$

Next we consider the expression $(\lambda sx.x)bc$ and substitute s for b and x for c. Since s doesn't appear in the expression, it's the same as replacing x for c, so $(\lambda sx.x)bc = c$ and consequently

$$\lambda bc.b((\lambda sx.x)bc) = \lambda bc.(b(c)).$$

This last expression, upon relabeling the variables, is the same as $\lambda sx.(s(x))$.

To summarize, we now have $0 = \lambda sx.x$ and $1 = S(0) = \lambda sx.s(x)$. In words, 1 is the function that has inputs two functions and applies the first function to the second, that is, it inputs s and x and calculates $s(x)$.

The number 2 is now defined as $S(1)$. This equals

$$S(\lambda sx.s(x)) = (\lambda abc.b(abc))(\lambda sx.s(x)).$$

I will leave it to the reader to check that this can be simplified to $\lambda sx.s(s(x))$. In words, the number 2 is the function that inputs two functions and applies the first function twice to the second function. In general, n is the function that has two inputs and applies the first function n times to the second function, that is, it inputs s and x and calculates $s(\ldots(s(s(x))))$.

Now that we have the natural numbers, we can define addition. This is done simply using the successor function. The sum of two numbers n and m is defined by[7]

$$m + n \equiv mSn.$$

To illustrate we will show that $1 + 1$ is indeed 2. We start with $1 + 1$.

$$1 + 1 = 1S1 = (\lambda sx.s(x))(\lambda abc.b(abc))(\lambda ty.t(y)).$$

In the first expression, we replace s by the second expression and x by the third expression. This gives

$$\lambda abc.b(abc)(\lambda ty.t(y)).$$

Replacing a by $(\lambda ty.t(y))$ gives

$$\lambda bc.b((\lambda ty.t(y))bc).$$

Finally replacing t and y by b and c, gives $\lambda bc.b(b(c))$ which is 2 (because we can change b to s and c to x).

At this point you probably agree with Gödel that Church's approach does not have the intuitive clarity of Turing's, but the λ-calculus builds on itself and does seem to become easier as its initial strangeness wears off. To illustrate, we will briefly describe how logical operations are handled.

Logic

In logic we have two values called *true* and *false*. These are denoted by T and F. The two basic logical operators are *and*, denoted by $\wedge$, and *or*, denoted by $\vee$. Given two statements p and q that are either true or false, the statement $p \wedge q$ is true only in the case when both p and q are true. This can be expressed as

$$T \wedge T = T, \quad T \wedge F = F, \quad F \wedge T = F, \quad F \wedge F = F.$$

The statement $p \vee q$ is true in every case except when both p and q are false, which can be expressed as

$$T \vee T = T, \quad T \vee F = T, \quad F \vee T = T, \quad F \vee F = F.$$

In the λ-calculus T is defined by $T \equiv \lambda xy.x$ and F by $F \equiv \lambda xy.y$, so both T and F have as input two expressions. T chooses the first expression while F chooses the second expression. (The observant reader will have noticed that the definition for F is the same as for 0.)

We look at certain concatenations. In each case the leftmost expression takes the next two expressions as input, so for example, for TTF, the leftmost T inputs T and F. Since T just outputs the first expression, we obtain $TTF = T$. It is straightforward to check each of the following:

$$\boldsymbol{TTF = T, \ TFF = F, \ FTF = F, \ FFF = F.}$$

This should be compared to the truth table for $\wedge$. (I made certain letters bold to help make this connection.) Consequently we can define $\wedge$ to be the function that inputs two functions and concatenates them and with an extra F added to the end. Therefore in the λ-calculus $\wedge$ is defined by[8]

$$\wedge \equiv \lambda xy.xy(\lambda st.t) = \lambda xy.xyF.$$

The observations

$$\boldsymbol{TTT = T, \ TTF = T, \ FTT = T, \ FTF = F,}$$

show that we can define $\vee$ to be the function that inputs two functions and puts a T between them. Consequently $\vee$ is defined by

$$\vee \equiv \lambda xy.x(\lambda st.s)y = \lambda xy.xTy.$$

From these beginnings a whole class of functions can be built. Surprisingly, these functions are exactly the same as the computable functions that can be built using Turing machines. We now turn to a completely different way of considering computation.

Tag Systems

Tag systems date back to Post's work back in the 1920s. He wanted to reduce statements in mathematics to strings of symbols, and proofs to manipulations on the strings. He considered what he initially thought would be an easy example, but he soon realized that things were far from straightforward.

A *tag system* is a rule for manipulating strings of symbols from a finite alphabet. At each stage letters are dropped from the beginning of the string and letters are added to the end. The system is defined by d, the number of letters that we drop, and strings associated to the letters. Each letter is *tagged* with its own special string. The starting string is replaced by doing two operations; the tag of the initial letter of the string is added to the end of the string, and the first d letters of the string are deleted. The computation keeps going if the resulting string has d or more letters in it. It halts when the number of letters drops below d.[9]

For example, suppose our alphabet just consists of the letters a and b, that a is tagged with the string ab and b with a and we delete the first two letters ($d = 2$). If we start with bb then our first step is to look at the first letter and read its tag. In this case it will give us a. We add this to the end of our initial string and drop the first two letters. This gives a. Since we only have one letter in the string the computation comes to an end.

If we start with the string $bbbb$, we get the following calculation that ends with a continuous repetition of ab.

bbbb

bba

aa

ab

ab

ab

Post considered the tag system with two letters *a* and *b*, where *a* is tagged with *aa*, *b* is tagged with *bbab* and the update rule drops the first three letters. He asked if it is possible to tell whether given an initial string the system would become repetitive. He found it "intractable." So did Minsky who looked at the system with the help of a computer. In fact, this question still remains unanswered.

In 1961, Minsky showed how any Turing machine can be emulated by a tag system. This means that given any algorithm, there is a tag system that computes it. This fact is sometimes expressed in the literature by saying that tag systems are *Turing complete*. It has even been shown that you only ever need to consider systems that drop the first two letters — 2-tag systems — to get Turing completeness.[10]

Given an algorithm, we can in theory design a Turing machine that implements it, and then convert to a tag system. However, the resulting tag system is usually extremely complicated. It would be nice to construct the tag system without first constructing a Turing machine. This has been done in certain cases. We will look at one particular example, an interesting tag system that was found by Liesbeth De Mol as part of her PhD. dissertation in 2007.[11] It is a very simple system that calculates the *modified Collatz function*.

The *Collatz function* is a function that takes a positive integer and gives another one. The function is described by two rules depending on whether the input number is even or odd. If you have an even number, then you divide it by two. If you have an odd number, you multiply it by three and add one to it. The *Collatz conjecture* is that if you start with any positive integer and keep applying the function you will eventually reach 1.

As an example, consider starting with 5. Since it is odd, we multiply by three and add one, which gives us 16. Since this is even, we divide by two, and we get 8. We keep dividing by two and eventually end with 1. As you may have surmised by its name, the Collatz conjecture is a conjecture. Nobody has a proof that it is correct or a counterexample to show that it is not. Many mathematicians worked on the problem in the 1960s. In fact, so many mathematicians were spending so much time on it that some joked that the Collatz conjecture had been designed to slow down mathematical research in the United States.

The modified Collatz function is based on the fact that three times an odd integer plus one must be even, so the Collatz function applied to an odd integer gives an even integer. The next stage is to divide this even integer by two. The modified Collatz function does these two steps at once.

The modified Collatz function, $f(n)$, takes positive integers. If the integer is odd, it multiplies it by three, adds one and halves the resulting number. If the integer is even, it divides the integer by two. So looking back at our example where we started with 5, the next number with the modified Collatz function is 8. (The Collatz function goes from 5 to 16 and then to 8.) Iterating f gives the sequence 5, 8, 4, 2 and finally 1.

De Mol constructed the following simple 2-tag system with three letters a, b and c. The tags are bc for a, a for b and aaa for c. At each stage, the tag of the first letter is added to the end of the string and then the first two letters are deleted. Positive integers are encoded as strings of all as. The number of as gives the integer, so the number 5 is encoded as $aaaaa$. Only strings that consist entirely of as correspond to integers. Strings that involve bs or cs are not given numerical value. They correspond to intermediate calculations. (I have given more information describing exactly how this tag system corresponds to the modified Collatz function in the notes.)[12]

We will run it for our example starting with the integer 5, denoted by $aaaaa$. The first letter of the string is a. This means that we add a's tag of bc to the end of the string and delete the first two letters at the beginning of the string, so we obtain $aaabc$.

The following shows the complete calculation. Whenever we have a string of all as we have an integer. In these cases I have written the corresponding number in the lefthand column.

<pre>
5   aaaaa
          aaabc
         abcbc
          cbcbc
           cbcaaa
            caaaaaa
8   aaaaaaaa
              aaaaaabc
               aaaabcbc
                aabcbcbc
                 bcbcbcbc
                  bcbcbca
                   bcbcaa
                    bcaaa
4   aaaa
                      aabc
                       bcbc
                        bca
2   aa
                          bc
1   a
</pre>

Since the Collatz conjecture is unsolved it is not known whether De Mol's system will halt for every initial string.

One-Dimensional Cellular Automata

A *one-dimensional cellular automaton* consists of an infinite tape divided into cells. Each cell can have one of a number of states. We will only look at cases where there are just two states, which we will denote by *white* and *black*. This means that the tape will be divided into an infinite number of cells, which we depict as squares, each of which is colored either black or white.

The computation takes place at discrete time intervals. The initial tape is given to us at time 0. It first gets updated at time 1, then at time 2 and so on. Even though it is really one tape that is evolving at each time interval, it is easier to describe each instance as a separate tape. Given a tape, the subsequent tape, one unit of time later, is given by an updating rule that for each cell looks at the state of that cell and the states of some of its neighbors on the initial tape and gives the cell's new state on the updated tape. In the cases we will look at, the updating rule will be based on the state of the cell and the states of the immediate neighboring cell on either side. For example, we could have a rule that says if a cell and its two neighbors have the same color at time t, then the updated cell color at the next time, $t + 1$, will be black; otherwise the cell color at the next time will be white. With this particular rule we will start ($t = 0$) with the tape that has just three cells that are black as in the picture below. (The cells to the right and left of the ones depicted are all white.)

At the next stage ($t = 1$) we will get the following tape. (Check that you agree that now all the cells to the left and right of those depicted are all black.)

It is easier to see what is happening if we draw a grid. The first row gives the initial tape. The second row gives the tape after its first update and so on. For our example, we obtain the following grid showing the initial tape and the next three iterations of the procedure.

The color of each cell in this picture is obtained by looking a the cell immediately above with its two neighbors. This gives a way of describing the updating function in terms of pictures. There are eight possibilities for the colorings of three consecutive cells. Each of these is listed.

For each of these possibilities, the updated middle cell color for the next step is drawn below. For our example we will have the following picture of the update function.

These pictures give a pictorial representation of the rule, but also emphasize how the calculations are completely *local*. To update a cell, you only need to know the states of three consecutive cells from the previous tape. This is quite unlike calculations involving Turing machines or the lambda calculus. For example, in the lambda calculus, there can be some distance from the lambda being expanded and the term it is being applied to; and for computations using Turing machines, the tape head often has to travel large distances. It is quite remarkable that cellular automata are computationally equivalent to these other systems — that anything computed by a Turing machine can be computed by a one-dimensional cellular automaton.

Though these pictures are a good way of representing the rules, there is a more succinct way that is often used. First, denote the black cells in the second rows by 1 and the white cells by 0. For our example, we look at the picture above. The leftmost "T" has a black base, so we denote this by 1. The next "T" has a white base, so we denote it by 0. Proceeding in this way, we obtain 10000001 as a concise description of all of the eight "T"s. We can then think of this as a number in binary

$$10000001 =$$

$$1 \times 2^7 + 0 \times 2^7 + 0 \times 2^5 + 0 \times 2^4 + 0 \times 2^3 + 0 \times 2^2 + 0 \times 2^1 + 1 \times 2^0$$

$$= 128 + 1 = 129.$$

There are a total of 256 rules for these cellular automata. The one we have looked at is called *Rule 129*.

Stephen Wolfram in his book *A New Kind of Science* gives an extensive description of cellular automata. We will look at one of the examples that he gives of a simple computation being done by one.

Consider *Rule 132*. For those whose binary is shaky, here is a picture of it.

We will run it on two starting tapes. One has five consecutive back cells and one has six consecutive black cells. We obtain the following pictures.

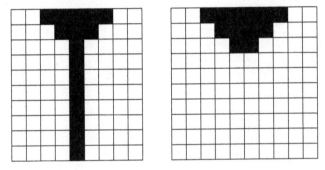

Given a string of consecutive black cells this rule keeps reducing the number of black cells by two until there are no cells left or one is left. There are two types of behavior. If the number of black cells in the initial string was odd, then one cell will stay black forever. If the number of black cells in the initial string was even, then eventually no black cells will be left. This rule can be thought of as telling us whether a number is odd or even.

One nice property of cellular automata is that we have a picture that shows the whole computation. Wolfram, in his book, looks at all 256 rules and classifies them into four groups depending on what can happen. Rules in group 1 have very simple behavior where the system stabilizes. Rules belonging to group 2 produce computations that oscillate. Group 3 rules produce chaotic looking calculations. Group 4 is the most interesting. This class of rules have calculations that show mixtures of chaos and stability. Wolfram conjectures that rules in this class are universal machines that have the ability to do any computation whatsoever. In the next chapter we will look at universal computers and will note that Matthew Cook proved that one of these, *Rule 110*, was universal.[13] It is an amazing result that something so simple can do any computation whatsoever.

6 Encodings and the Universal Machine

"A man provided with paper, pencil, and rubber, and subject
to strict discipline, is in effect a universal machine."
Alan Turing

After looking at various forms of computation we return to Turing's paper. To re-cap where we are: Turing needed to give a formal definition of algorithms, and he does this in terms of what we now call Turing machines. The Church-Turing thesis says that if we are presented with any algorithm it is possible to construct a Turing machine that performs the algorithm.

Because Turing machines are called machines we tend to think of these diagrams as depicting physical machines. Indeed, given a concrete example of a Turing machine and a tape, I can almost hear a little click as it changes states, and then a satisfying clunk when it enters the accept state, but the important fact about these machines is that they are describing algorithms. Turing has found an elegant way of giving complete descriptions of algorithms.

When you are given a description, you can often say exactly the same thing, but using completely different words. This is what Turing does next. He takes his machines and shows that all the information given by the diagram of a Turing machine can be encoded into a string of 0s and 1s. The algorithm that is exactly described by a picture of a Turing machine is now exactly described by a string of binary digits.

If you have any experience with programming, you know that programs are usually written in a high-level language using words in English, but to run the program it needs to be converted by the computer into a string of 0s and 1s. Turing machines can be thought of as programs. Thinking of them in this way makes it seem fairly natural to try to convert our diagrams of Turing machines into binary strings that we call *encodings*, and this is what we do in this chapter. It might not be clear at the moment why we would want to do this, but it is one of the most important ideas in the theory of computation. We will see that encodings lead naturally to the idea of a universal computer. Then in the following chapters we use encodings and a famous argument of Cantor to show the limitations on computations.

The idea of converting algorithms into binary strings might seem fairly natural to us today, but in Turing's day it was not. Turing got the idea of encoding his machines from the work of Kurt Gödel who, for his work on the incompleteness theorems, had encoded statements in mathematics into strings of numbers. Gödel's numbering is a clever idea that is useful in logic, but it is not widely used in other parts of mathematics. Turing borrowed the concept and applied it to algorithms. In the process the idea changed from being rather obscure to being one of the fundamental ideas behind the modern computer. It was Turing who first realized that an algorithm and data could both be encoded as a single string of numbers.

A Method of Encoding Finite Automata

We will give an encoding for finite automata. Finite automata are simpler than Turing machines and so are simpler to encode. This means that the process of converting from the diagram to the string is quicker, and that the resulting string is shorter. Though finite automata are simpler than Turing machines, we use exactly the same ideas to encode them. Once you have seen how to encode one machine you should be able to devise a method of encoding any machine.

We will assume the input alphabet just consists of 0s and 1s. (If the input string uses different alphabet, it could be converted to one just using 0s and 1s.)

To give a complete description of a finite automaton you need to list the following information:

1. The number of states.

2. The start state.

3. The accepting states.

4. For each state, what happens if a 0 is input and what happens if a 1 is input.

To help with our description, we will assume that our states are numbered, and that the first state is the start state.

We now need a way to encode the description as a binary string. The key idea is to use the 0s to encode numbers and the 1s to encode the other information. This other information is analogous to punctuation. In a written language you need punctuation to tell us where sentences start and end, and to separate clauses. We need to do the same for our descriptions of machines. We will use four 1s in a row at the start and end of our encoding. Three 1s in a row will denote the end of a category — think *period*. Two 1s in a row will denote a change of subcategory — think *semicolon*. One 1 will be used much like a *comma*. A concrete example will make all of this clear. We will consider the machine M_2 that we have considered before. It is redrawn in figure 1. The only difference in the diagram is the name of the states. Before they were labeled with letters, but we will now always label the states with consecutive integers, starting with 1 for the start state.

We begin and end our encodings with four 1s, so the first four symbols in the encoding are 1111. The next thing we need to input is the number of states. This machine has three states which we encode as three 0s, so the encoding begins 1111000. We have finished talking about the number of states, so we add 111. The next thing to enter a list of accept states. In this case, just state 3 is accepting, which we denote by three 0s. Our encoding now begins 1111000111000. Again we add three 1s to indicate we have finished talking about accept states, which gives 1111000111000111.

If both states 2 and 3 had been accept states, we would have entered this information as 0011000. The two 1s separating the descriptions of

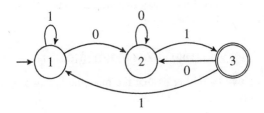

Figure 1

M_2: Strings that end with 01.

the states. If all three had been accept states, we would have entered 0110011000 into the block describing the accept states.

We return to the example. We now need to give information about what happens when we are in a state and either 0 or 1 is input. We go through each state in turn. For each state we first say which state is entered when a 0 is input and then which state is entered when a 1 is input — using a single 1 to separate these pieces of information.

In state 1, if 0 is entered we move to state 2, if 1 is entered we move to state 1. This is encoded as 0010. In state 2, if 0 is entered we move to state 2, if 1 is entered we move to state 3. This is encoded as 001000. In state 3, if 0 is entered we move to state 2, if 1 is entered we move to state 1. This is encoded as 0010. Each of these three pieces of information are separated by two 1s. This gives 001011001000110010. This is now added to the encoding we have so far, to obtain 111100011100011100101100100011001. Finally, we add four 1s to indicate that we have finished the description. The final encoding is 11110001110001110010110010001100101111.

The standard notation for the encoding of a machine M is $\langle M \rangle$, so

$$\langle M_2 \rangle = 11110001110001110010110010001100101111.$$

It is important that we can not only encode a finite automaton and obtain a string of 0s and 1s, but that we can also decode the string. We should not only be able to go from M to $\langle M \rangle$, but should also be able to convert $\langle M \rangle$ back to M. It is possible to do this with our method of encoding. To illustrate, consider the string 1111001110011100101101001111. We will go through the decoding of this example in a step by step way.

The first four 1s just say that we are beginning a description of a machine, and the last four 1s say that we are ending the description. We now read off the first substring of 0s.

1111**00**1110011100101101001111

There are two 0s telling us that the machine has two states. The next substring of 0s

11110011100**00**11100101101001111

tells us that state 2 is the accept state. The next bolded substring

1111001110011**10010**1101001111

tells us that in state 1 if we receive a 0 we move to state 2 and if we receive a 1 we move to state 1. Finally the bolded substring

11110011100111001011**01001**111

tells us that in state 2 if we receive a 0 we move to state 1 and if we receive a 1 we move to state 2. This is a complete description of the finite automaton. It is drawn in figure 2. This machine, M_9, is one that recognizes strings with an odd number of 0s.

Universal Machines

If we are to do an actual computation, we need an input string in addition to the finite automaton. We can incorporate this in our encoding by just tacking it on at the end. If we are given a machine M and an input string I, we will let $\langle M, I \rangle$ denote the concatenation of the string $\langle M \rangle$ followed by the input string I. Suppose for example, that someone gives us the string below that is an encoding of an automaton and input string and wants to know whether the answer to the computation is accept or reject.

$$\langle M, I \rangle = 1111001110111001011010011111110010110$$

We know that the encoding of the machine is given before the input string. We also know that the machine encoding begins and ends with four 1s, so the second time we see four 1s we know that the machine

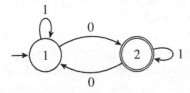

Figure 2

M_9: Strings with an odd number of 0s.

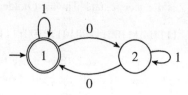

Figure 3

Machine for strings with an even number of 0s.

encoding has ended and that input string is about to begin. Consequently, it is easy to distinguish the two parts. In the example we have

$$\langle M \rangle = 1111001110111100101101001111 \text{ and } I = 110010110.$$

As before, we can now decode the machine encoding and draw the machine. I have done this and drawn it in figure 3. It is the same as the previous machine, but with the first state as the accepting state instead of the second.

This machine accepts strings that have an even number of 0s. We are inputting the string 110010110, which has four 0s, so the machine accepts it. Hence the answer to the computation

$$\langle M, I \rangle = 1111001110111100101101001111110010110$$

is accept, or yes.

To recap what we have done, we know how to take a finite automaton M and input data I and then encode both pieces of information as one string $\langle M, I \rangle$. We know that we can also reverse the process. Given the string $\langle M, I \rangle$, we have a method separating $\langle M \rangle$ from I, then reconstructing the original automaton M, and finally, running the string I on our re-construction of machine M.

This seems a really roundabout way of doing things, but there is an important idea here. Let me repeat the last sentence of the previous paragraph with one change: Given the string $\langle M, I \rangle$, we have an *algorithm* for separating $\langle M \rangle$ from I, then reconstructing the original automaton M, and finally, running the string I on our re-construction of machine M. By the Church-Turing thesis, if we have an algorithm, then we can construct a Turing machine to perform the algorithm, so there is a Turing machine that will accept $\langle M,I \rangle$ as input, then simulate the machine M on its input I. The conclusion is that there is one Turing machine that can simulate any finite automaton running any input. This is clearly a powerful machine, but we can build something even more powerful.

We have looked at finite automata, but we can encode Turing machines in much the same way. The only difference is that Turing machines are more complicated and need a little more information to describe them, which results in longer encodings. As with finite automata, there is an algorithm for re-constructing the Turing machine from its encoding.

As a consequence, if we are given an encoding $\langle M,I \rangle$ for a Turing machine M and an input I, we know that there is an algorithm that reconstructs M and then runs I on the reconstruction of M. As before, this can be re-stated as given an encoding $\langle M,I \rangle$ there is an algorithm that will take $\langle M,I \rangle$ as input and give the answer *accept* if M accepts I, give the answer *reject* if M rejects I and, never come to an end if M does not halt on I.

Now by the Church-Turing thesis we know that there exists a Turing machine for every algorithm, so we obtain:

There is a Turing machine, U, that will take any $\langle M,I \rangle$ as input and give the answer accept *if M accepts I, give the answer* reject *if M rejects I, and never halt if M does not halt on I.*

This machine U is able to simulate any Turing machine on any input. Machines that can do this are called *universal Turing machines*.

Modern computers are universal Turing machines. (There is a slight technicality here concerning the finite memory of a computer. We will say a little more about this later.) We can think of M as representing a program and I as the data. Then $\langle M,I \rangle$ corresponds to the program and data after both have been converted to binary strings. When the computer runs $\langle M,I \rangle$ it simulates running the program M on the input I.

Construction of Universal Machines

A universal machine is a computer that can take a description of both a Turing machine and its input string and then can simulate running the machine on the string. First, let us briefly consider humans and our capabilities.

In the chapter on Turing machines we considered a machine that looked at strings of 0s and 1s and decided whether it had an equal number of each. We then looked at an example of running the machine on the string 001.

The description of the machine was given by a diagram. From this description and the input string 011, we simulated running the machine. This might have been done entirely in our heads or we might have had to write intermediate steps on paper, but in either case our brains simulated running the machine on its input. By the end of the chapter, we saw that given any diagram, or any other way of completely describing a Turing machine, and an input string, we can simulate running the machine on the input. At the time we thought that we were learning about how Turing machines worked, but in the process we saw that we had the ability to emulate any Turing machine on any input. This ability means that we are universal Turing machines. We have the ability to run any algorithm whatsoever.

Saying that we are universal Turing machines may initially sound as though we are saying something wonderful about our abilities, but this is not really the case. It essentially boils down to the fact that if we are given a list of instructions that tell us exactly what to do in every situation, then we have the ability to follow it. Looking back at the examples in the previous chapters, once you understood what the pictures and descriptions of Turing machines meant, it became easy to simulate running a machine on an input string. There was hardly any brainpower involved. At each stage there was just one thing that had to be done next. Consequently, universal Turing machines are not necessarily complex, highly intelligent machines. They can be relatively simple things.

In the previous section we considered a universal Turing machine U taking $\langle M, I \rangle$ as input and then running M on the input I. The machine U can be quite simple and it is often the case that M is much more complicated. In other words, it can be harder to design an algorithm than to design a machine to run it.

By now you are probably wondering if it is possible to draw a diagram of a universal Turing machine. The answer is that it is, but a fair amount of work has to be put in to explain exactly what each state of the machine is doing.

We won't go through the many details required to construct a universal Turing machine, but for readers who really want to look further into this, I suggest finding a copy of Marvin Minsky's book *Computation: Finite and Infinite Machines* where he gives several examples. There is a trade off between the number of states, the number of different symbols allowed on the tape, and the difficulty in following why everything works. His first example has twenty three states and uses six symbols on the tape. This is the easiest one to follow, because the states are grouped into various sections that perform certain specific functions. He then gives an example which has just seven states and uses four symbols, but he warns "... as the reader will see, that machine, or any like it, would be unsuitable for expository purposes."

Instead of constructing a universal Turing machine explicitly, we will adopt a slightly indirect route. We will show that present day computers are universal machines and then show that they can be represented by Turing machines.

This approach has the advantage that it makes the Church-Turing thesis seem much more plausible. This thesis says that given any algorithm, a Turing machine can be constructed that performs the algorithm. Once we have shown that the computational equivalence of modern computers and Turing machines, the thesis can be re-stated as: *Given any algorithm, a modern computer can be programmed to compute it.* This version seems quite believable.

Modern Computers Are Universal Machines

To show that a computer is a universal Turing machine we must show that the computer can simulate any Turing machine on any tape. This seems entirely reasonable, but we will sketch an outline of how this can actually be proven.

For humans, it helps to have diagrams representing Turing machines, but for computers, it is better to describe the machines without using pictures. Fortunately, this is easy to do.

For example, when we introduced Turing machines, we started with the following diagram.

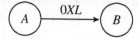

The picture tells you that if you are in state *A* and receive input 0, then you move to state *B*, write *X* on the tape and move the tape head left. We could have given the same information with a quintuple $(A, 0, B, X, L)$, where the first entry is the current state; the second entry is the current tape symbol; the third is the new state; the fourth tells what is written on the tape; and the last entry tells in which direction the tape head moves. (This representation using quintuples is in fact the standard notation. Turing didn't draw diagrams; he used these quintuples.)

Once you have described the machine by a list of quintuples it is fairly easy to write a computer program that simulates the machine on an input tape. The program reads in the list of quintuples and the input string. At each stage the program reads the current state and current input symbol. Then it searches through the list of quintuples to find the one with first two entries that agree. It then uses the next three entries to update the state, update the stored string and select the next input symbol.

This argument is rather brief, but it gives the outline of how any Turing machine running any input can be simulated on a computer. It shows that modern computers are universal machines. (There is one slight technicality. Recall that we allowed Turing machines to have infinite tapes. The tape only ever contains finitely many non-blank symbols, but this number, though finite, could possibly be enormous. When we simulate the machine on a modern computer we do need to assume the computer has enough storage to be able to do the calculation.)

That we can simulate Turing machines on modern computers is not surprising. What is surprising is that we can design a Turing machine to simulate a modern computer, showing that Turing machines are equivalent in computing power to modern computers. We will sketch how this is done. The first step is to get a concrete description of the modern computer.

Von Neumann Architecture

Later we will talk more about John von Neumann, but it is important to know a few facts before we proceed. The *First Draft of a Report on the EDVAC* is probably the most important paper on the design of modern computers. It was written in 1945, as the first electronic computers were being built. It described the basic outline of how a computer should be designed, incorporating what had been learned from the design of earlier machines.

This paper has a very different point of view to that of Turing's paper. Turing was interested in what it was possible to compute. His machines were theoretical constructs meant to incorporate the basic computational steps of human computers. Von Neumann was interested in building a physical machine. His focus was not on the theory of computation, but on the design of an efficient machine for doing actual computations. The resulting design outlined in the report is often referred to as von Neumann architecture and most modern computers are based on this architecture.

Von Neumann's design built on the ideas of many people. The *First Draft*, as its name suggests, was a draft of a paper and it was only meant to be circulated to a small number of people. The fact that von Neumann was listed as the sole author and that other people's work was not credited correctly would not have been a problem if the readership was restricted, as originally intended, to just a few colleagues, but the *First Draft* was widely circulated and became enormously influential in the design of all subsequent computers. Some of the originators of the ideas contained in the paper, notably J. Presper Eckert and John Mauchly, were quite understandably upset that they received no credit for their substantial contributions to what is now known as von Neumann's architecture. That said, some of the key ideas were von Neumann's. One example is the stored-program concept, which dates back to when von Neumann realized the importance of Turing's paper. We will discuss more of the history in a later chapter, but first let us describe the architecture.

The heart of the computer is the central processing unit (CPU). The CPU loads an instruction from memory which it then decodes and executes. This might involve reading more data from memory and might involve performing simple arithmetic and logical operations. The CPU consists of a *control unit* and an *arithmetic and logic unit* (ALU). Both of these units contain specialized and fast memory cells called *registers*. One special register is the *program counter* (PC). Its role is to keep track of the address of the next instruction to be executed. At the start of each cycle the control unit reads the address of the next instruction from the PC and then loads the instruction from the memory cell with that address.

Part of the design of the architecture is the *instruction set*. These instructions list the operations of the CPU at the most basic level. The instructions include the rules for moving data between memory and the registers. They also include a few simple operations using arithmetic and logic. Any program that a computer can run has to be converted into a list of these primitive machine instructions. We normally write programs using a high-level language, but before a computer can implement them, they have to be run through a *compiler* to convert them into machine language.

In determining what is theoretically computationally possible with a modern computer we need a mathematical model that contains all the essential features, but none of the unnecessary complications involved in running an actual physical machine. One model is the *Random Access Machine* (RAM) that we describe below.

Random Access Machines

The Random Access Machine is a theoretical model of a machine with von Neumann architecture. This model, though theoretical, captures all the fundamental properties of actual computers with this architecture, and so is a good model for describing most modern machines.[1]

The acronym RAM has two meanings: the most common meaning is *Random Access Memory*; the lesser known meaning, and the one we will be using, is *Random Access Machine*. However, these ideas are related. All computers have a list of things stored in memory. Each of these things has an address that tells the computer where in the memory it is stored. If the memory is random access, then each of these addresses can be located immediately. The computer doesn't have to search through a long list to find a particular location.

Turing machines use their tapes to store information. These machines are far from having random access. If the machine needs to use a piece of information that is stored far from the cell that the tape-head is currently reading, then the head has to move through all the intermediate cells before the information can be read. The Random Access Machine, as we shall see, has a random access memory. If it needs a piece of information, it can go immediately to the address where it is stored.

The RAM has an infinite number of *memory cells*, denoted

$$M(1), M(2), M(3), \ldots,$$

and a finite number of of *registers*, denoted by

$$R_0, R_1, \ldots, R_r.$$

Each memory cell and each register can store an integer.

There is also a *program counter* (PC) that can hold non-negative integer values.

The machine runs a program consisting of a list of instructions with the program counter giving the number of the next instruction to be implemented. The instruction set is quite simple. Each instruction tells how the register R_0 and the program counter should be updated. Since the list of instructions is fairly short we will list them all.

The first three instructions involve loading numbers into the registers. We can load an integer n into R_0, load the number stored in any of the registers into R_0, and load the number stored in R_0 into any register. We will denote these three operations by

$$R_0 := n, R_0 := R_s \text{ and } R_s := R_0.$$

We can do simple arithmetic operations. We are allowed to add a number n to the value currently stored in R_0, to add the number in any other register to the value currently stored in R_0, and to multiply the number in any other register to the value currently stored in R_0. We will denote these operations by

$$R_0 := R_0 + n, R_0 := R_0 + R_s, \text{ and } R_0 := R_0 \times R_s.$$

We can also read the number stored in any memory location into R_0, and we are allowed to write whatever is in R_0 to any memory location. These can be written as

$$R_0 := M(R_s) \text{ and } M(R_s) := R_0,$$

where $M(R_s)$ means first read the integer that is stored in R_s and then use this as the address of the memory location.[2]

The program counter normally increases by one after an instruction has been read. This means that after the machine has read an instruction it goes to the next instruction on the list, but we can modify the program counter in various ways. The program can jump to the nth instruction, which we will denote by

$$PC := n.$$

We are also allowed two conditional statements that involve whether or not the number stored in R_0 is zero. These are

$$\text{if } R_0 = 0, \text{ then } PC := n,$$

and

$$\text{if } R_0 > 0, \text{ then } PC := n.$$

When we start a computation, the numbers contained in the registers and memory are all set to zero. The input consisting of a string of numbers representing both the program and data is read into memory. If the input string is k units long, it is read into $M(1), M(2), \ldots, M(k)$ and the rest of the memory cells remain at zero. The program counter is set to one.

The RAM provides an excellent model of the modern computer. Modern computers, at the most basic level, do computations based on a small number of simple operations and these operations are essentially the ones listed in the description of the RAM. Consequently, to show that a modern computer can be simulated by a Turing machine, it is sufficient to show how to simulate a RAM.

RAMs Can Be Emulated by Turing Machines

As we have noted before, it is fairly straightforward to construct Turing machines to add and multiply integers. An adding machine would input the integers m and n and then leave the integer $m + n$ on its tape when its computation is completed. Once we have machines that can add and multiply, we can combine them into one Turing machine that has the ability to do both addition and multiplication. Just as subroutines are used in programming, we can incorporate Turing machines that do simple functions into more complicated machines that need to use those simple functions. Our Turing machine that is going to simulate a RAM will need to both add and multiply numbers. We will assume that we have constructed machines to do these operations and can incorporate them into our new machine as we build it.

We have already commented that we cannot make Turing machines more powerful by giving them more features. In particular, giving them more tapes and tape heads does not increase the computational power. The way this is proved is by showing that any Turing machine with multiple tapes can be emulated by Turing machines with one tape.[3] We will use this fact. Our first step will be to convert our RAM to a Turing machine with multiple tapes. Once we have done this, we can convert it to a machine with just a single tape.

Our initial Turing machine will have one tape for the memory, one tape for each of the registers and the program counter, and one additional tape for scratch work. First we describe the memory tape.

The RAM starts by inputting a string that lists the data and instructions. We will let $v_1 v_2 \cdots v_k$ denote it this string. The Turing machine needs to keep track of the position of each symbol in the string — it needs to keep track of the subscripts. To do this we add to the alphabet two new symbols that we will denote by

$$\# \text{ and } *.$$

Then we initialize our Turing machine by taking the input string $v_1 v_2 \cdots v_k$ for the RAM and inserting symbols to obtain

$$\#1 * v_1 \#2 * v_2 \#3 * v_3 \# \cdots \#k * v_k \#$$

on the memory tape. This makes sure that we can keep track of the number assigned to each instruction. For example, if we need to find the second element of the original RAM input string, we can look along the new string for #2*. Once we see this, we know that v_2 is going to be the next string. We know that the string v_2 starts immediately after seeing #2* and ends just before we see the next #.

The other tapes initially are all blank, except for the program counter tape which has the number 1 on it.

We will give an example of the Turing machine in action. Suppose that it has been running and we now observe it after it has already completed nine instructions. We will see how it deals with the tenth. After it finishes an instruction the machine reads the number of the next instruction to be executed from the program counter tape. We will assume that the first nine instructions did not involve jumps and that the program counter was just updated by one at each stage. Consequently, the program counter will have 10 written on it. The machine searches through the memory tape looking for #10. It finds #10 * v_{10}#. Next it examines v_{10}. This might be an integer that corresponds to an instruction. Let us suppose that it corresponds to the instruction $R_0 := M(R_3)$. The machine then reads the integer on the R_3 tape and then looks for this integer on the memory tape. Suppose, for example, that R_3 contains the integer 41. The machine then looks for #41* on the memory tape. It finds #41 * v_{41}# and copies v_{41} to the R_0 tape. Finally, it adds one to the integer contained on the program counter tape. The tenth instruction is complete and it begins the eleventh.

In a similar way, all of the other machine instructions for the RAM can be implemented on our Turing machines with many tapes.

Finally, as we noted, it is possible to emulate our machine with many tapes by a new machine that has only one tape. Of course, the resulting Turing machine would have many states and be rather complicated. It would also take many steps to perform one simple RAM instruction. However, we are not interested in actually constructing the machine. We just want to show that it can be done in theory. Once we are convinced that we can emulate each basic instruction of the RAM by a Turing machine, we know that we can then emulate the entire RAM. From this it follows that Turing machines have the computational power of modern computers.

Other Universal Machines

We have seen that modern computers are universal machines, but there are some very simple computation systems that are also universal. Minsky studied Post's tag systems and was able to construct one that simulated a universal Turing machine. Consequently, anything a Turing machine, or computer, can do a tag system can do — at least in theory.[4]

When we looked at one-dimensional cellular automata, we made the observation that some of the rules could be considered as algorithms for computations. Surprisingly, they can also simulate universal Turing machines. Stephen Wolfram conjectured that *Rule 110* was Turing complete. This is one of the rules that shows a mixture of chaos and stability depending on the starting tape. For some starting tapes the rule produces very simple output. For other starting tapes the output looks chaotic. Wolfram's conjecture was that *Rule 110* should be able to do any computation whatsoever. Here is the rule:

Matthew Cook, who was working at Wolfram Research at the time, managed to prove that Wolfram was correct. This is an impressive result. It it is not at all clear how, given a computation, we should design a starting tape so that *Rule 110* performs it. How did Cook prove his? The first step was to use the fact Turing machines can be emulated by a certain class of tag systems. Then he showed that these tag systems could be emulated by *Rule 110*.

Of course, this is a theoretical result. It is hard to imagine that a practical computer could be constructed using this rule.[5] But it is quite remarkable that something so simple can be a universal computer.

However, as we have already observed, in general it's not the universal computer that is complicated, but the programming. In the case of *Rule 110* we can show that it can simulate any other cellular automaton by choosing the initial tape configuration correctly. Though in practice, there is not an easy way to go from an algorithm to the construction of the correct initial tape, the important point is that even though it might be hard, it can be done. We know that for any algorithm there definitely is some cellular automaton that implements the algorithm and there is some input tape for *Rule 110* that simulates the computation of this automaton.[6]

What Happens When We Input ⟨*M*⟩ into *M*?

Given a machine M we know that we can encode it as a string $\langle M \rangle$. We know that we can construct a universal Turing machine U that takes $\langle M, I \rangle$ as input and then simulates running M on input I. It is natural to ask what happens if we run a machine on its own encoding. What happens when we input $\langle M \rangle$ into M, or equivalently, what happens when we input $\langle M, \langle M \rangle \rangle$ into U? It is not at all clear that this is going to be the least bit useful, but we will see a little later a practical example where this can occur, and it does seem a natural question to explore. Let's look at a few examples.

We saw that

$$\langle M_9 \rangle = 1111001110011100101101001111.$$

This machine is depicted in figure 2 and, as we have already seen, this machine accepts strings with an odd number of 0s and rejects strings with an even number. The encoding $\langle M_9 \rangle$ has ten 0s, so if we run M_9 on $\langle M_9 \rangle$, the machine will reject it. An equivalent way of saying exactly the same thing is that if we input $\langle M_9, \langle M_9 \rangle \rangle$ into U, it will end with *reject*, where

$$\langle M_9, \langle M_9 \rangle \rangle =$$

11110011100111001011010011111111001110011100101101001111.

For our second example, consider M_2. This is the machine that accepts strings that end in 01. We know that the encoding of any machine ends with four 1s, so $\langle M_2 \rangle$ will end with four 1s and so will be rejected by M_2.

Finally consider M_3, which is re-drawn in figure 4. This machine accepts strings with an even number of 1s. Encoding gives

$$\langle M_3 \rangle = 1111001110111010011001011111.$$

Since this has an even number of 1s, M_3 will accept $\langle M_3 \rangle$.

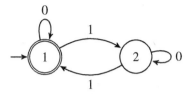

Figure 4

M_3: Strings with an even number of 1s.

This idea of self-reference will turn out to be an important one, as we will see, but first let us see an actual example of why we might run a machine (or algorithm) on its own encoding.[7]

As we previously commented, we usually write our programs using a high-level language, but to actually execute them they must first to be converted to machine language. This conversion is done by a compiler. Suppose that our current compiler is not very efficient and we decide to write a new compiler that is going to minimize the amount of time that the compiled programs will take to run. We will denote the code for our optimized compiler by Q. Since we have written Q in a high-level language it will need to be run through our current compiler before the computer can execute it. We will let the compiled version of our compiler be denoted by Q'. However, we don't just want a compiled version of Q, but an optimized compiled version of Q, so we should compile Q using Q'. This results in the optimized, compiled version of Q which we will denote by Q''. Now suppose that we designed Q in such a way that it can also optimize machine code in subsequent passes, then we would run Q'' on Q'' in order to get the double-optimized, compiled version of Q.[8]

At this point it is probably still not clear that running a machine on its encoding is important, but we will see shortly that it is precisely this idea that leads to some of the most unexpected and beautiful results in the theory of computation.

7 Undecidable Problems

We now return to decision problems. As we noted before, a decision problem is a question that depends on input parameters. Once we have given values to the input parameters it becomes a question that has either *Yes* or *No* as the answer. We also said that a decision problem was *decidable* if there exists an algorithm that gives the correct answer in every case, and *undecidable* if such an algorithm doesn't exist.

Turing wanted to show that a general solution to Hilbert's Entscheidungsproblem — to find an algorithm for every decision problem — was not possible. He needed to construct a decision problem that he would be able to prove was undecidable. This is the theme of this chapter. We will give some decision problems and will prove that there are no Turing machines that can decide them.

At the end of the last chapter we were looking at whether or not machines would accept their encodings. If we state the question a little more clearly, we can see that we have a decision problem. In fact, we can state this as two decision problems by first asking about finite automata and then asking about Turing machines. These two decision problems are:

1. Given a finite automaton, will it accept its encoding?
2. Given a Turing machine, will it accept its encoding?

Consider the first problem. Can we construct an algorithm that, given any finite automaton, decides whether or not the automaton will accept its encoding? The answer is clearly yes. Given any finite automaton, we have an algorithm to give its encoding. We can then run the automaton with its encoding as input. We know that the process will stop after a finite time. It either stops in an accept state, in which the answer to the problem is yes, or it stops in some other state, in which case the answer is no. We have a simple algorithm that always gives the correct answer, so this decision problem is decidable.

What about the second decision problem? At first glance it looks as though we could give exactly the same argument to show that it, too, is decidable, but there is a problem. In the argument we used the fact that when we run a finite automaton on any input it will always halt (the number of steps equals the length of the input string). However, we saw that there are three possibilities for the eventual behavior of a Turing machine: it can halt in the accept state, halt in the reject state, or never halt. It's not clear from what we have done so far whether the third possibility, never halting, is really necessary. It seems plausible that a Turing machine that never halts could just be a problem of a poorly designed algorithm and that if we had designed it better we would have a machine that would always halt. Unfortunately, this is not the case. As we will see, the problem of machines not halting is not something that can be designed away. There are questions that we can ask that cannot be answered correctly in every case by machines that always halt. We will stop considering the second decision problem for the moment, but we will return to it later and show that it is undecidable.

In addition to the second decision problem, we will also show that it is not possible to design an algorithm to tell whether a computer program halts or runs forever — *the halting problem*.

The proofs we give use two key ideas. One is *proof by contradiction*, which is a method of proving a statement by assuming its negation and then deriving a contradiction. The other key idea really comes from Georg Cantor's diagonal argument, but we will give it in terms of a paradox that was first stated by Bertrand Russell. Since many readers may not have seen proofs by contradiction, we will begin by explaining how they work. We will illustrate the method by giving the classical proof that the square root of two is not a rational number.

Proof by Contradiction

In all proofs we are trying to prove some statement is true. We will let P stand for the statement we want to prove. There are two basic type of proof — direct and indirect. In direct proofs, we start with statements that we know are true and then give a logical argument in which each step in the argument follows logically from earlier steps. The argument then concludes with the proposition P that you want to prove. In a proof by contradiction, an indirect proof, we argue in a different way.

We want to prove that P is true, but we begin the argument by assuming that P is false. We then proceed as before, with each step following logically from the steps before. The final step in the proof occurs when we derive a contradiction — that is, show some statement is both true and false. Since we are assuming that mathematics is consistent and there are no statements that are both true and false, something must be wrong with our proof. Our argument is watertight, with each line following from the ones above, so the only possible place that it could have gone wrong is in the assumption that P is false. Consequently, P must be true.

Proof by contradiction may seem a little convoluted initially, but it is a very powerful tool that is often used in mathematics.[1] Our goal is to prove that there is no algorithm that decides the second decision problem. That is we must show the non-existence of an algorithm. Proofs by contradiction are often useful in proofs in which you want to show something does not exist. To illustrate, we will give an important example, the proof that the square root of two is not a rational number, but first we need to recall the definition of the integers and rational numbers.

The integers consist of zero and the positive and negative whole numbers. The usual notation for the integers is $\mathbb{Z}$, coming from the German word *zahlen* to count, so we can write:

$$\mathbb{Z} = \{\cdots -2, -1, 0, 1, 2, \ldots\}.$$

The rational numbers are fractions with an integer in the numerator and a positive integer in the denominator. The usual notation for rational numbers is $\mathbb{Q}$, from quotient.[2] We will write:[3]

$$\mathbb{Q} = \{m/n : \text{where } m, n \text{ belong to } \mathbb{Z} \text{ and where } n > 0\}.$$

Given a rational number m/n we can always put in lowest form by canceling common factors from both the numerator and denominator. If we are presented with 17/34, we can cancel top and bottom to get the fraction 1/2. When the fraction is in lowest form, it goes without saying that it is not possible to find a common factor that can be cancelled from both the denominator and numerator. (This is an obvious fact, but we will need it in our proof.)

We will also need to use the fact that if the square of an integer is even, then the original integer was even. This follows from the facts that if you square an even number then you obtain another even number, but if you square an odd number you obtain another odd number.

We are now in a position to prove that the square root of two is not a rational number, so P is the statement that $\sqrt{2}$ *is not a rational number*. We are going to use a proof by contradiction. This means we will start by assuming P is false and then derive a sequence of consequences that finally results in a contradiction — a statement that is both true and false. Saying that the statement $\sqrt{2}$ *is not a rational number* is false is the same thing, once you get rid of the double negative, as saying that $\sqrt{2}$ *is a rational number*.

Proof. 1. This is a proof by contradiction, so we start by assuming that $\sqrt{2}$ is a rational number.

2. This means that $\sqrt{2} = m/n$, for some positive integers m and n.

3. The integers m and n might have common factors, but we can always reduce to lowest form, so we know we can write $\sqrt{2} = p/q$, for some positive integers p and q, where p and q have no common factors.

4. We can square both sides of the equation in the line above to give $(\sqrt{2})^2 = (p/q)^2$ or $2 = p^2/q^2$.

5. Multiplying by q^2 gives $2q^2 = p^2$.

6. Clearly $2q^2$ is an even number. Therefore p^2 must be even.

7. Since p^2 is even, it must be the case that p is even.

8. So p is divisible by 2, which means that we can write $p = 2k$, where k is the integer obtained by dividing p by 2.

9. Substituting $p = 2k$ into (5) gives $2q^2 = (2k)^2$.

10. Consequently, $2q^2 = 4k^2$.

11. Canceling 2s gives $q^2 = 2k^2$.

12. Since $2k^2$ is even, q^2 must be even, and so q must be even.

13. Lines (12) and (7) show that both p and q are even, which means that they have a common factor of 2.

14. Line (3) states that p and q have no common factors.

15. It is a contradiction to say that p and q have no common factors and that they do have common factors.

16. Since we have derived a contradiction, there must be an error somewhere. The only place that an error could have been introduced was at the beginning when we assumed that $\sqrt{2}$ is a rational number, so this must be false. Consequently, it must be true that $\sqrt{2}$ is not a rational number

□

The proof is often said to show that $\sqrt{2}$ is irrational, but it doesn't do that. It proves that $\sqrt{2}$ is not a rational number. (Exactly the same proof, if we allow p to be negative, can be used to show that $\sqrt{-2}$ is not a rational number.) To show that $\sqrt{2}$ is irrational, you need to have an argument that shows that $\sqrt{2}$ is a real number. Then once you know it is a real number, but not rational, you can deduce that it is irrational.

Russell's Barber

Russell used an argument of Cantor to show that the naive definition of a set was flawed. Later we will look at what both Russell and Cantor did, but Russell invented a paradox to help explain the underlying argument in a simple way. We can phrase Russell's "Barber Paradox" as a proof by contradiction:

Imagine that there is a man who needs to shave regularly and is a barber; that there is a town where all the men who live there either regularly shave themselves or regularly get the barber to shave them. Suppose that we are also told that the barber shaves every man in town who does not shave himself and does not shave any man in town who does shave himself.

Carefully read the paragraph above and think about what we can deduce about where the barber lives.

We will give a proof that he doesn't live in town. It's another proof by contradiction.

Proof. This is a proof by contradiction, so we start by assuming the barber lives in the town.

There are two possibilities. Either the barber shaves himself or he does not. We will consider each in turn.

If the barber shaves himself, then he is man who lives in town who shaves himself, but we are told the barber does not shave any man who lives in town who shaves himself — a contradiction.

If the barber does not shave himself, then he is a man who lives in town who does not shave himself, but we are told the barber shaves every man who lives in town who does not shave himself — a contradiction.

We started with the assumption that the barber lived in the town and showed that this always led to a contradiction. This means that the assumption is false and so we have proved that the barber does not live in town. □

Now let us return to the statement of the problem and add a sentence saying that the barber lives in the town. We now have:

Imagine that there is a man who needs to shave regularly and is a barber. Imagine that there is a town where all the men who live in the town either regularly shave themselves or regularly get the barber to shave them. Suppose we are told that the barber shaves every man who lives in the town who does not shave himself and does not shave any man who lives in the town who does not shave himself. Suppose, in addition, that the barber lives in the town.

We now have a problem. Our previous argument showed that the barber cannot live in town and we have now added a contradictory statement saying that the barber does live in town. We now have a genuine paradox. And this is how the Barber's Paradox is usually given. However, this is not the form that is useful or that we need. Consider one more modification to the question.

Can there exist a man such that all of the following statements are true?

1. *He is a man who needs to shave regularly and is a barber.*
2. *There is a town where all the men who live in the town either regularly shave themselves or regularly get the barber to shave them.*

3. *The barber shaves every man who lives in the town who does not shave himself and does not shave any man who lives in the town who shaves himself.*

4. *The barber lives in the town.*

This question has a simple answer. No. The barber does not exist.

The next section has arguments of exactly this type. If we don't specify whether or not the barber lives in the town, there is no problem with the barber existing and living outside the town. If we insist that the barber lives in the town, then we are forced to the conclusion that he doesn't exist.

Finite Automata That Do Not Accept Their Encodings

At the end of the last chapter we looked at the finite automaton M_9 and showed that it rejected its encoding $\langle M_9 \rangle$. We also showed that M_2 rejected its encoding $\langle M_2 \rangle$, but that M_3 accepted its encoding $\langle M_3 \rangle$. This tells us that there are two types of finite automata: those that accept their encodings and those that do not. We can now ask whether there is a machine M_{FA} that will tell us exactly which finite automata do not accept their encodings. The machine M_{FA}, if it exists, will only accept encodings of finite automata that do not accept their encodings, so M_{FA} will accept $\langle M_9 \rangle$ and $\langle M_2 \rangle$, but not $\langle M_3 \rangle$. We will now prove that M_{FA} cannot be a finite automaton.

Proof. This is a proof by contradiction, so we start by assuming that M_{FA} is a finite automaton.

There are two possibilities. Either M_{FA} accepts $\langle M_{FA} \rangle$ or it does not. We will consider each in turn.

If M_{FA} accepts $\langle M_{FA} \rangle$, then it is a finite automaton that accepts its encoding, but by definition M_{FA} only accepts encodings of finite automata that do not accept their encodings — a contradiction.

If M_{FA} does not accept $\langle M_{FA} \rangle$, then it is a finite automaton that does not accept its encoding, but by definition M_{FA} accepts encodings of finite automata that do not accept their encodings — a contradiction.

We started with the assumption that M_{FA} is a finite automaton and showed that this always led to a contradiction. This means that the assumption is false and so we have proved that M_{FA} cannot be a finite automaton. □

This proof may seem a little confusing at first, and it should probably be read very slowly and carefully, but it is exactly the same proof that was given in the previous section showing that the barber did not live in the town. Machines correspond to men. Machines that don't accept their encodings correspond to men who do not shave themselves. Machines that are finite automata correspond to men that live in town.

In the last section we proved that the barber could not live in town, but this leads to the question, does he live elsewhere? We can ask the corresponding question. Could M_{FA} be a Turing machine? The answer is, of course, yes. We have shown that there is an algorithm for deciding whether or not finite automata accept their encodings. Consequently, there is a Turing machine that does this.

Turing Machines That Do Not Accept Their Encodings

We now turn our attention to Turing machines and look at whether or not they accept their encodings. Just as with finite automata, there are Turing machines that accept their encodings and there are Turing machines that don't. One difference from the previous case is that we know that if a finite automaton does not accept its encoding, then it has rejected its encoding, but with Turing machines there are three possible outcomes. Being told that a Turing machine does not accept its encoding does not imply that the Turing machine has rejected its encoding. It could be the case that the machine never halts on its encoding. This possibility, that the machine diverges, will turn out to be extremely important when looking at what Turing machines can and cannot do.

However, Russell's barber argument can be used in exactly the same way to show that there is no Turing machine that will only accept encodings of Turing machines that don't accept their encodings.

Proof. This is a proof by contradiction, so we start by assuming that the Turing machine M_{TM} exists.

There are two possibilities. Either M_{TM} accepts $\langle M_{TM} \rangle$ or it does not. We will consider each in turn.

If M_{TM} accepts $\langle M_{TM} \rangle$, then it is a Turing machine that accepts its encoding, but by definition M_{TM} only accepts encodings of Turing machines that do not accept their encodings — a contradiction.

If M_{TM} does not accept $\langle M_{TM} \rangle$, then it is a Turing machine that does not accept its encoding, but by definition M_{TM} accepts encoding of Turing machines that do not accept their encodings — a contradiction.

We started with the assumption that M_{TM} existed and have shown that this always led to a contradiction. This means that the initial assumption is false and consequently we have proved that M_{TM} does not exist.

□

This proof shows that there is no algorithm that will tell us whether or not a Turing machine will reject its encoding. This means the question *Given a Turing machine, will it not accept its encoding?* is undecidable. The negation in the middle of this question makes it rather convoluted, but there is an observation that will make things look a little simpler.

Suppose we have a decision problem P that is decidable. Then it is possible to design a Turing machine that always halts. It halts in the accept state if the answer is yes and halts in the reject state if the answer is no. If we then take this Turing machine and interchange the accept and reject states we will end up with a machine that decides the negation of P. This observation means that if a decision problem is decidable, then so is its negation. This observation also implies that if a decision problem is undecidable, then its negation must be undecidable.[4]

Consequently, we have proved that the decision problem *Given a Turing machine, will it accept its encoding?* is undecidable.

The good news is that we have found a question that is undecidable and we have proved it is undecidable. This is important because it is a proof of the existence of an undecidable problem. Hilbert believed that there were no undecidable problems, and we now have a proof that he was wrong.

However, our decision problem seems rather convoluted and not particularly pertinent to the sort of questions we really want to ask about computers and programming. Fortunately, it doesn't require much more work to obtain some undecidable questions that are much more relevant.

Does a Turing Machine Diverge on Its Encoding? Is Undecidable

When we run a Turing machine on an input string there are three possible outcomes: it halts in the accept state; it halts in the reject state; or it never halts. Let us look at three questions related to this.

1. Is it possible to construct a Turing machine that receives encodings of Turing machines as input and halts in the accept state only if the encoded Turing machine accepts its encoding?

2. Is it possible to construct a Turing machine that receives encodings of Turing machines as input and halts in the accept state only if the encoded Turing machine rejects its encoding?

3. Is it possible to construct a Turing machine that receives encodings of Turing machines as input and halts in the accept state only if the encoded Turing machine diverges on its its encoding?

The answer to the first question is *Yes*. We can construct a Turing machine A that takes $\langle M \rangle$ as input and then simulates running the Turing machine M on the input $\langle M \rangle$. Consequently, if M ends in an accept state, then A accepts $\langle M \rangle$. If M ends in a reject state, then A rejects $\langle M \rangle$. If M diverges on $\langle M \rangle$, then the simulation will also never halt and so A will diverge on $\langle M \rangle$, so our machine A will always stop in the accept state whenever M accepts $\langle M \rangle$.

The answer to the second question is also *Yes*. We can construct a Turing machine B by taking A and interchanging the accept and reject states. This means B takes $\langle M \rangle$ as input and then simulates running $\langle M \rangle$ on M. If M ends in an accept state, then B rejects $\langle M \rangle$. If M ends in a reject state, then B accepts $\langle M \rangle$. If M diverges on $\langle M \rangle$, then the simulation will also never halt and so B will diverge on $\langle M \rangle$. This means our machine B will always stop in the accept state whenever M rejects $\langle M \rangle$.

The answer to the third question is *No*. We will prove this. Again it is a proof by contradiction.

Proof. This is a proof by contradiction, so we will assume that a Turing machine C exists that receives encodings of Turing machines as input and halts in the accept state if and only if the encoded Turing machine diverges on its encoding.

We will now describe a new Turing machine D that consists of B and C running in parallel. Given any encoding of a Turing machine $\langle M \rangle$ run it on B and C simultaneously. If either B or C accepts $\langle M \rangle$, then D accepts $\langle M \rangle$. If neither B or C accepts $\langle M \rangle$ and at least one of them rejects it, then D rejects $\langle M \rangle$. If both B and C diverge on $\langle M \rangle$, then so will D.

The machine D receives encodings of Turing machines as input. It halts in the accept state only if B or C halts in the accept state, but this happens if the encoded machine rejects or diverges on its input. This means that D halts in the accept state only if the encoded machine does not accept its encoding. However, this gives a contradiction, as we have shown that there is no Turing machine with this property.

The conclusion is that there is no Turing machine that receives encodings of Turing machines as input and halts in the accept state only if the encoded Turing machine diverges on its its encoding.

$\square$

This shows that the question *Does a Turing machine diverge on its encoding?* is undecidable. Again, the negation will also be undecidable, so we know that the question *Does a Turing machine halt on its encoding?* is undecidable.

The Acceptance, Halting, and Blank Tape Problems

We now have two undecidable questions: *Does a Turing machine accept its encoding?* and *Does a Turing machine halt on its encoding?* We will generalize both questions.

The acceptance problem: *Given any Turing machine M and any input I, does M accept I?*

The halting problem: *Given any Turing machine M and any input I, does M halt on I?*

Then we will consider a variation of the halting problem.

The blank tape problem: *Given any Turing machine M and a blank input tape, does M halt?*

Let's begin by looking at the acceptance problem. Can we construct a Turing machine that takes as input both an encoding $\langle M \rangle$ of any Turing machine and any input I, and design it in such a way that it halts in the accept state whenever M accepts I and halts in the reject state whenever M does not accept I? The answer is clearly no, since we cannot design such a machine for the more restricted case where the input I is $\langle M \rangle$. If we cannot design a machine that decides the easier question, then there is no way that we will be able to design a machine that decides a harder question that includes the easier question as a special case, so the acceptance problem is undecidable.

Similarly, the halting problem is more general that asking if a given Turing machine halts on its encoding, so the halting problem is also undecidable.

We can restate the halting problem as asking whether there exists an algorithm that takes programs and data as input and tells us whether the program will halt on the data. As we have shown, this question is undecidable. This is far from just being an academic curiosity. It would be very beneficial to computer programers if they had a tool that would tell them that their program would never halt on some input, but there isn't.

However, if we restrict the class of programs and data under consideration, the question might become decidable. We might be able to design an algorithm that doesn't belong to the restricted class that decides the question. We might be able to find a barber who doesn't live in town.

The final decision problem that we will consider is the blank tape problem. This initially looks like a special case of the halting problem — the input tape is now always blank, but there is a trick that shows that if you could find a decision procedure for the blank tape problem, then you would have a decision procedure for the halting problem. Since the halting problem is undecidable, no such decision procedure can exist. Here's the trick.

Given any Turing machine M and any input I, you can construct a new Turing machine M_I. This new Turing machine, when presented with a blank tape, first writes I on the tape and then emulates M running on input I. The machine M_I will halt on a blank tape if and only if the machine M halts on I. There is nothing deep going on here, and you might be wondering why this problem is even worth mentioning, but, as we shall see, this problem has some interesting consequences.

An Uncomputable Function

Turing machines have a linear tape for their input and for writing. If we restrict the machine to having just one tape, the tape-head does a lot of scuttling back and forth along the tape during a computation. The Hungarian mathematician Tibor Radó decided to investigate the maximum amount of 'scuttling' that the head can do before it reaches the accept state.

In 1962, Radó invented the *busy beaver function* based on this idea. Actually, he invented several slightly different functions based on the same basic ideas. The one that is easiest to work with is called the *maximum shifts function*, denoted $S(n)$.

We will look at Turing machines that are only allowed to write two symbols. These are usually denoted by 1 and 0, where 0 also stands for the blank symbol. The machines aways start with a blank tape. We want to know how the number of steps a machine takes until it halts relates to the number of states of the machine. Let us make this idea a little more precise.

We will denote the number of states of the Turing machine by n. (Following Radó, the accept state and the reject state are not counted in this number.) Given all Turing machines with n states, some will halt on a blank tape and some will not. Of those that halt, there must be at least one machine that takes the most number of steps until it halts. We let $S(n)$ denote this maximum number of steps.

This function $S(n)$ is well-defined. To calculate it for a given n, you need to construct all Turing machines that have n states and then run them on a blank tape. You then need to count the number of steps until they halt. The largest number of steps taken gives you the number $S(n)$. The problem with this procedure is that some machines will take a long time to halt and others will never halt. If a machine has been running for a long time and hasn't halted, how can you tell which class it belongs to? However, despite this problem, $S(n)$ is known for some values of n:

$$S(1) = 1, S(2) = 6, S(3) = 21, S(4) = 107.$$

Surprisingly, these are the only known values.[5] It is known that $S(5) \geq 47,176,870$ and that $S(6) > 7.4 \times 10^{36,534}$. As you can see, even though we don't yet know many exact values, these numbers are growing rapidly. In fact it can be shown that $S(n)$ grows faster than any computable function.[6] We won't show this, but we will show that $S(n)$ is not a computable function.

Recall that a function $f(n)$ is a computable function if we can find a Turing machine that outputs $f(n)$ when we input any natural number n. Equivalently, we can say that $f(n)$ is a computable function if there is an algorithm that that computes $f(n)$ given n.

If $S(n)$ were a computable function, then we would be able to give a procedure for deciding the blank tape problem along the following lines: Given any Turing machine M with a blank tape, first count its number of states, n, and then calculate $S(n)$ using the algorithm that computes it. Then start running M. It might halt after a certain number of steps, but if after $S(n)$ steps it still hasn't halted, you will know that it will never halt. Consequently, if $S(n)$ is a computable function, then the blank tape problem is decidable. Since we have shown that the blank tape problem is not decidable, it must be the case that $S(n)$ is not a computable function.

Turing's Approach

The halting problem is a decision problem concerning arbitrary programs and arbitrary input data. It is the question that asks whether or not the program will halt on the data. The fact that this question is undecidable means that there is no algorithm that will decide the question correctly in every case. The halting problem is probably the most well-known undecidable decision problem. However, this is not the problem that Turing described in his paper.

As Turing described his machines, they did not have accept states. They were designed to compute real numbers and so would never stop if computing an irrational number. The notion of a Turing machine was changed to include accept states by Stephen Kleene and Martin Davis. Once you had this new formulation of a Turing machine, you could consider the halting problem. Davis[7] gave the halting problem its name.

The halting problem is easy to comprehend if you already understand terms like 'program' and 'input,' and what it means for programs to halt on their inputs. These concepts are familiar to us because of the ubiquity of computers nowadays, but in 1936 computers had not been invented. The halting problem is hard to describe to someone who has not seen or heard of a computer. Turing did not want an undecidable problem that concerned properties of a hypothetical computing device. He wanted an undecidable problem that was immediately comprehensible to mathematicians. He found one using an ingenious argument of Georg Cantor.

8 Cantor's Diagonalization Arguments

"I see it, but I don't believe it!"
Georg Cantor

"I don't know what predominates in Cantor's theory —
philosophy or theology, but I am sure that there is no
mathematics there."
Leopold Kronecker

"No one shall drive us from the paradise which Cantor has
created for us."
David Hilbert

Georg Cantor 1845–1918

Georg Cantor moved with his family from St. Petersberg to Germany when he was eleven years old. After completing his dissertation at the University of Berlin in 1867 he took up a position at the University of Halle where he remained for his professional life.

Cantor was interested in the notion of 'size' for sets; especially infinite sets. His ideas are highly original, and he proved some startling results; one of which is that there are an infinite number of ever larger infinities. Like Frege, Cantor used an intuitive idea of a set. He realized that the set of all possible sets caused problems for his theory, but the question was whether there was some slight modification that could be made to fix things, or whether there was some substantial error that would require a major modification of what mathematicians were doing.

The quotes at the start of this chapter give some idea of how Cantor's work was initially received. Some mathematicians thought his work was nonsense. Leopold Kronecker and Henri Poincaré both attacked it. He was even attacked on religious grounds. If God was the infinite, did having different infinities imply an infinite number of gods? Other mathematicians, notably Hilbert, supported Cantor and felt that what he was doing was not only correct, but important for the future of mathematics.

In the first chapter, we discussed the foundations of mathematics. There was the *formalist* approach of Hilbert and the *logicist* approach of Russell and Whitehead. The logicists wanted to show that all of mathematics could be derived from logic. The formalists wanted a formal system in which you could construct arguments about the consistency and completeness of the axioms. Both approaches assumed that there was nothing fundamentally wrong with mathematics. The paradoxes that had cropped up in Cantor's work could be eliminated with a more careful definition of a set.

However, another group of mathematicians took a completely different view. They regarded the work of Cantor as being seriously wrong, so wrong that the foundations of mathematics should be rewritten specifically to exclude the types of arguments that Cantor was using. These were the *intuitionists* founded by the Dutch mathematician, L. E. J. Brouwer around 1908.

Cantor was probably bipolar, and he took many of the attacks on him very personally, and had to be hospitalized at various times during his life. He was especially hurt by Kronecker's reaction. Kronecker had been his teacher, and Cantor held him in great respect. However, Kronecker believed that Cantor's ideas were completely wrong and that Cantor was corrupting both mathematics and other mathematicians. He was both very public and very harsh in his comments about Cantor and his work.

Nowadays, the view of most current mathematicians is that Cantor was right, and most would agree with Hilbert's words: "No one shall drive us from the paradise which Cantor has created for us."

Cardinality

Cantor asked what it meant for two sets to have the same size. For finite sets this is just the question of counting the number of elements in the sets, so $\{a, b, c\}$ and $\{1, 2, 3\}$ have the same size because they both have three elements, but Cantor wanted to extend the idea of size to infinite sets. He decided to use the idea of a *bijection*.

A bijection between two sets A and B is a pairing of elements in A with elements in B in such a way that each element of A is paired with exactly one element of B and such that each element of B is paired with exactly one element of A — each element of one set has a unique partner in the other set. Cantor then defined two sets to have the same *cardinality* if it is possible to find a bijection between them. If it is impossible to find a bijection between two sets, then they don't have the same cardinality.

We will use the absolute value notation to denote the cardinality of a set, so $|A|$ stands for the cardinality of A. If the sets A and B have the same cardinality, we will write $|A| = |B|$.

We often use function notation to describe bijections, so for the example with $A = \{a, b, c\}$ and $B = \{1, 2, 3\}$, we could define a function $f : A \to B$ by $f(a) = 1, f(b) = 2$ and $f(c) = 3$. This means that a is paired with 1, b with 2 and c with 3. Each element of A and B has a unique partner in the other set, so the function f describes a bijection. Since we have given an explicit bijection between A and B we have proved that they have the same cardinality and so we can write as $|A| = |B|$. For finite sets this is not particularly exciting. It doesn't seem that we are saying anything important. The cardinality of finite sets just corresponds to the number of elements that are in the set, so, for our example, we can write $|A| = |B| = 3$.

Let us now turn our attention to infinite sets where things get much more interesting. We know that the even natural numbers are strictly contained[1] within the natural numbers; the natural numbers are strictly contained within the integers; the integers are strictly contained within the rational numbers; and the rational numbers are strictly contained within the real numbers. We can denote this symbolically by:

$$2\mathbb{N} \subset \mathbb{N} \subset \mathbb{Z} \subset \mathbb{Q} \subset \mathbb{R}.$$

It is obvious that cardinality cannot decrease if we add more elements to a set so we obtain:

$$|2\mathbb{N}| \leq |\mathbb{N}| \leq |\mathbb{Z}| \leq |\mathbb{Q}| \leq |\mathbb{R}|.$$

With finite sets, if you add more elements, then you increase the number of elements in the set and so the cardinality must increase. Surprisingly, this need not be true for infinite sets. We will show that

$$|2\mathbb{N}| = |\mathbb{N}| = |\mathbb{Z}| = |\mathbb{Q}| < |\mathbb{R}|.$$

Subsets of the Rationals That Have the Same Cardinality

To show that two sets have the same cardinality we have to show that there is a bijection between them. We first want to prove that $|2\mathbb{N}| = |\mathbb{N}|$. To do this we must construct a bijection $f:\mathbb{N} \to 2\mathbb{N}$, that is, a way of pairing elements in $\{1, 2, 3, 4, \dots\}$ with elements in $\{2, 4, 6, 8, \dots\}$. This is fairly easy to do. Consider the function f defined by $f(n) = 2n$. This pairs the number n in $\mathbb{N}$ with the even number $2n$ in $2\mathbb{N}$. Given a number in $\mathbb{N}$, you double it to find its partner in $2\mathbb{N}$. Given a number in $2\mathbb{N}$, you halve it to find its partner in $\mathbb{N}$. Clearly, this is a bijection, and so we have proved that

$$|2\mathbb{N}| = |\mathbb{N}|.$$

This might seem surprising when you first see it. Clearly $\mathbb{N}$ contains more elements than $2\mathbb{N}$. It not only contains all the even natural numbers, but also the odd ones. It would seem that the cardinality of $\mathbb{N}$ should be twice the cardinality of $2\mathbb{N}$. This is in fact true, but we will see that doubling an infinite cardinal number does not give a larger cardinal. Multiplying an infinite cardinal number by two gives back the same infinite cardinal.

This is a very curious property of infinite sets that is definitely not true for finite sets. Given an infinite set A, it is always possible to find a subset B, that doesn't contain every element of A, but in such a way that the cardinality of B is exactly the same as the cardinality of A. This means that every element of A is paired with a distinct element of B. The first time one sees this it seems counterintuitive, but that is because our intuition is based on finite sets where it cannot occur. This property is now an accepted part of mathematics, but it is easy to see why Cantor's ideas weren't immediately accepted.

Cantor gave a name to the cardinality of the natural numbers. He denoted it by $\aleph_0$.[2] Our bijection above between the natural numbers and the even numbers shows that

$$|2\mathbb{N}| = |\mathbb{N}| = \aleph_0.$$

A similar argument can be used to show that the cardinality of the odd natural numbers is also $\aleph_0$.

If A and B are disjoint sets, that is sets that don't contain any elements in common, then $|A \cup B| = |A| + |B|$. In the example with $A = \{a, b, c\}$ and $B = \{1, 2, 3\}$ we have $A \cup B = \{a, b, c, 1, 2, 3\}$. Notice that $|A \cup B| = 6 = 3 + 3 = |A| + |B|$. For finite sets this is all very straightforward, but now let us return to infinite sets. Let A equal the even natural numbers and B the odd natural numbers. The sets A and B are disjoint. Their union is $\mathbb{N}$. We know that $|A \cup B| = |A| + |B|$, but this says that $\aleph_0 = \aleph_0 + \aleph_0$. This strange looking statement is true.

This shows that we have to be very careful when dealing with cardinals. They do not behave like ordinary numbers. Cardinal addition is done the way we have described, and though it leads to strange statements like

$$\aleph_0 = \aleph_0 + \aleph_0 = \aleph_0 + \aleph_0 + \aleph_0 = \aleph_0 + \aleph_0 + \aleph_0 + \aleph_0,$$

it does not lead to any contradictions.

We have shown that $|\mathbb{N}| = |2\mathbb{N}| = \aleph_0$. Now we will show that the cardinality of all of the integers is also $\aleph_0$. As we noted before, the integers consist of the positive and negative whole numbers along with zero. The natural numbers — the positive whole numbers — have cardinality $\aleph_0$. The negation of the natural numbers — the negative whole numbers — will also have cardinality $\aleph_0$. The set containing just 0 has cardinality 1. This means that the cardinality of the integers, $|\mathbb{Z}|$, is $\aleph_0 + \aleph_0 + 1$. It is clear that

$$\aleph_0 + \aleph_0 \leq \aleph_0 + \aleph_0 + 1 \leq \aleph_0 + \aleph_0 + \aleph_0.$$

But we know that both $\aleph_0 + \aleph_0$ and $\aleph_0 + \aleph_0 + \aleph_0$ equal $\aleph_0$, and, consequently, we can replace both the left and right sides of the inequalities with $\aleph_0$ to obtain

$$\aleph_0 \leq \aleph_0 + \aleph_0 + 1 \leq \aleph_0.$$

This shows[3] that $\aleph_0 + \aleph_0 + 1$ is also equal to $\aleph_0$, and finally we deduce that $|\mathbb{Z}|$ is $\aleph_0$. We now have

$$|2\mathbb{N}| = |\mathbb{N}| = |\mathbb{Z}| = \aleph_0.$$

The next step is to show that the cardinality of the rational numbers is also $\aleph_0$. We start by looking at the positive rational numbers $\mathbb{Q}^+$. Since the positive rational numbers contain the natural numbers as a subset we can deduce that their cardinality is greater than or equal to $\aleph_0$, that is, $|\mathbb{Q}^+| \geq \aleph_0$.

We will now show that $|\mathbb{Q}^+| \leq \aleph_0$. As we did before, we can restrict our attention to $p/q \in \mathbb{Q}^+$ where p and q have no common factors, so, for example, we will not use $5/10$, but will use $1/2$. (This is to ensure that we will only have one representative for each rational.) We define a function

$$f \colon \mathbb{Q}^+ \to \mathbb{N}$$

by $f(m/n) = 2^m 3^n$, so, for our example, $f(1/2) = 2^1 3^2 = 18$.

This function is certainly not a bijection, because numbers like $5 \in \mathbb{N}$ don't have a corresponding partner in $\mathbb{Q}^+$, but notice that every element of $\mathbb{Q}^+$ has a partner in $\mathbb{N}$ and that no two elements of $\mathbb{Q}^+$ share the same partner. Consequently, we have found a bijection between $\mathbb{Q}^+$ and a proper subset of $\mathbb{N}$, which implies that $|\mathbb{Q}^+| \leq \aleph_0$.

We have shown $\aleph_0 \leq |\mathbb{Q}^+| \leq \aleph_0$. From this we obtain $|\mathbb{Q}^+| = \aleph_0$. Consequently, we now know

$$|2\mathbb{N}| = |\mathbb{N}| = |\mathbb{Z}| = |\mathbb{Q}^+| = \aleph_0.$$

Next, we give an argument similar to the one we gave for the integers. The rational numbers consist of the positive rationals, the negative rationals and 0. We have shown that $|\mathbb{Q}^+| = \aleph_0$. Clearly the negative rational numbers have the same cardinality as the positive ones. As before, we obtain $|\mathbb{Q}| = \aleph_0 + \aleph_0 + 1 = \aleph_0$.

To summarize, we have shown that

$$|2\mathbb{N}| = |\mathbb{N}| = |\mathbb{Z}| = |\mathbb{Q}| = \aleph_0.$$

We have also shown that

$$\aleph_0 + \aleph_0 + \cdots + \aleph_0 = n\aleph_0 = \aleph_0.$$

Rational numbers have the form p/q. There are $\aleph_0$ choices for the numerators and $\aleph_0$ choices for the numerator, so the number of rational numbers is $\aleph_0 \times \aleph_0$, but we have shown that the cardinality of the rationals is $\aleph_0$. This means that

$$\aleph_0^2 = \aleph_0.$$

We can keep multiplying by $\aleph_0$ to deduce that

$$\aleph_0^n = \aleph_0$$

for any natural number n.

At this point you might be wondering if anything of importance is going on. It might look as though we have just replaced ∞ with a fancy symbol and have a complicated way of saying obvious things like the union of two infinite sets is another infinite set. This would be a valid comment if it couldn't be shown that there were other larger infinities, however, as we shall see, Cantor showed that there are an infinite number of larger infinities. But before get to this, we will describe Hilbert's Grand Hotel. This example is due to George Gamow and appears in his book *One Two Three ... Infinity: Facts and Speculations of Science*. There are now several versions of the story, sometimes it is presented as a paradox, but it is not. It is a version of Cantor's work on the addition of cardinal numbers.

Hilbert's Hotel

Hilbert's hotel is a hotel with an infinite number of rooms. These are numbered 1, 2, 3, and so on. On Monday night the hotel is full. Every room has someone staying in it. Suddenly there is a phone call to the manager from someone who needs a room for the night. The manager starts to explain that there is no room and that they are fully booked when the intern interrupts and explains how everyone, including the new arrival, can have a room. She tells everyone who is currently staying in the hotel to move to the room with the next largest room number, so if you are staying in room 102 you now have to move to room 103. Everybody who is currently has a room will get a new room, but room 1 will be freed up for the new arrival.

Though this might seem strange, there is nothing paradoxical about it. It is really a proof that

$$\aleph_0 + 1 = \aleph_0.$$

Everybody who is staying Monday night is also staying for Tuesday night. On Tuesday, ten people suddenly arrive and need rooms. It should be clear what to do to accommodate everyone. Move everybody who currently has a room to one with a number ten higher. The person who got moved on Monday from room 102 to room 103 now moves to room 113. This frees up rooms 1 through 10 for the new arrivals.

This argument can be extended to any finite number of new arrivals and shows that

$$\aleph_0 + n = \aleph_0$$

for any natural number n.

We have only been describing one of Hilbert's hotels. He has another one on the other side of town. It also has an infinite number of rooms and everyone is also occupied. Unfortunately, on Wednesday the building inspector finds that the hotel has been built on shaky foundations and declares it unfit for habitation. The infinite number of people staying there need a new place to stay. The manager of the condemned hotel calls the manager of the original hotel and asks if he has an infinite number of vacancies. The managers turn to the intern who again provides a solution. Everyone in the first hotel moves from their current room to the one that has number twice their current one. The poor person who was moved from room 102 to 103, then to 113 now gets moved to room 226. Everybody who was currently staying in the first hotel gets a new room with an even number. Now all the odd number rooms are free for the people from the condemned hotel. The intern tells the people in the condemned hotel who want rooms in the first hotel to multiply their old room number by two and to subtract one. This will be their new room number in the first hotel. The person who was staying in room 102 in the second hotel gets moved to room 203. In this way everybody gets a room.

This is an argument that shows

$$\aleph_0 + \aleph_0 = \aleph_0.$$

Subtraction Is Not Well-Defined

We have shown that $\aleph_0 + 1 = \aleph_0$, $\aleph_0 + \aleph_0 = \aleph_0$ and it is clear that $\aleph_0 = \aleph_0$. We have three equations. You might be wondering about the cardinality $\aleph_0 - \aleph_0$. Can't we rearrange the three equations listed above to obtain $1 = \aleph_0 - \aleph_0$, $\aleph_0 = \aleph_0 - \aleph_0$ and $0 = \aleph_0 - \aleph_0$? There seems to be a problem. We obtain different values for $\aleph_0 - \aleph_0$. This is true. Though addition for cardinals makes sense, subtraction does not. We say that subtraction is not well defined. The same is true of multiplication and division. Multiplication is well-defined with the product of two cardinals having a unique answer in every case, but division is not well-defined for infinite cardinals. Because there is no unique right answer for problems involving subtraction and division these two operations will be avoided. We will stick to addition and multiplication.[4]

General Diagonal Argument

Cantor had shown that $n\aleph_0 = \aleph_0$ and that $\aleph_0^n = \aleph_0$ for any natural number n. He then looked for a way to construct larger cardinals.

He started by considering the set of all possible subsets of a set. For example, the set $S = \{0, 1, 2\}$ has a number of possible subsets. These are the set $S = \{0, 1, 2\}$ itself; the subsets with two elements $\{0, 1\}$, $\{0, 2\}$ and $\{1, 2\}$; the subsets with one element $\{0\}$, $\{1\}$ and $\{2\}$; the subset with no elements $\{\}$. The set of all subsets of a set S is called the *power set* and denoted $\mathcal{P}(S)$. For our example,

$$\mathcal{P}(S) = \{\{0, 1, 2\}, \{0, 1\}, \{0, 2\}, \{1, 2\}, \{0\}, \{1\}, \{2\}, \{\}\}.$$

Observe that $|S| = 3$ and that

$$|\mathcal{P}(S)| = 8 = 2^3 = 2^{|S|}.$$

For finite sets S it is always true that $|\mathcal{P}(S)| = 2^{|S|}$. The reason for this is that when constructing subsets from a set S, there are two choices for each element, either to include or to exclude it. For our example, we might use I to stand for include and E for exclude. A string EIE would stand for excluding the first and third elements but including the second element, so in our example it would represent the subset {1}. The eight possible strings of length three using I and E are III, IIE, IEI, EII, IEE, EIE, EEI and EEE. It should be clear how each of these eight strings corresponds to each of the eight subsets.

Cantor extended this idea to infinite sets. We consider the underlying set to be the natural numbers and look at the set of all subsets of $\mathbb{N}$. When constructing a subset, there are two choices of whether to include or exclude 1, two choices for 2, two choices for 3 and so on. Consequently, we end up with a total of $2^{\aleph_0}$ subsets, so $|\mathcal{P}(\mathbb{N})| = 2^{\aleph_0}$.

Cantor proved a number of theorems but the following theorem is the one that bears his name.

Cantor's theorem
Given any set S, $|S| < |\mathcal{P}(S)|$.

Cantor's theorem tells us that $|\mathbb{N}| < |\mathcal{P}(\mathbb{N})|$ and consequently $\aleph_0 < 2^{\aleph_0}$. We now have an infinite cardinal that is larger than $\aleph_0$.

If we let $A = \mathcal{P}(\mathbb{N})$ then we can look at the set of all possible subsets of A. This will have cardinality $2^{2^{\aleph_0}}$. Cantor's theorem tells us that $|A| < |\mathcal{P}(A)|$ which means that $2^{\aleph_0} < 2^{2^{\aleph_0}}$. Proceeding in this way, we obtain an infinite number of ever larger infinite cardinals.

This is where Cantor realized that everything was not quite right. Consider the set of all possible sets. It is the largest set possible and so its cardinality will be the largest possible cardinal. Then what is the cardinality of the power set of the set of all sets? Cantor's theorem shows this has a larger cardinal. But now we have a paradox. We have found a cardinal number that is larger than the largest cardinal number!

From the modern perspective, sets are defined in such a way as to rule out the set of all sets. There is no largest set, and there is no largest cardinal. The paradox that Cantor found can be taken as a proof that there is no largest cardinal.

We will now prove Cantor's theorem. The proof uses the Barber's Paradox idea, but it should be remembered that Cantor was the originator of this argument, not Russell. First we give an example that will help to illustrate the idea behind the proof.

Imagine that there is a town with a population of exactly 1,000 people. The mayor of the town likes compiling lists of the residents. She has some lists that just have one or two people on them, some with many people and perhaps even an empty list on which she hasn't written any names. At the end of a mammoth list writing exercise, she realizes that she has written exactly one thousand lists. Since she has a thousand lists and the population is 1,000, she decides to give one list to each person. She does this by randomly sending a list to each person in town.

Everyone in the town looks at the list they were given, some people look at their list and see their name and they are pleased that the mayor had thought to include them on their list. Others look at their list and realized that their name isn't on it. They are disappointed. The town is divided into two factions: the happy people whose lists named themselves, and the disgruntled whose lists omitted their names.

The mayor, seeing that she has a group of disappointed people, decides to make a list of their names. She compiles a list of people who have been sent lists that did not include their names. She then looks at this new list and wonders if it listed exactly the same names as one of the thousand lists that she had already sent out. Is the list of disgruntled people a new list, or is it one of the thousand original lists?

She reasoned that if it was the same list as one that she had sent, then someone would have received this list of disgruntled people and looked at it. She imagined the person reading the list. There were two possibilities. If the person's name was on the list, then they would be happy at seeing their name, but this was a list of the disgruntled and so the name could not be on the list, so this possibility couldn't occur. On the other hand, if the person's name was not on the list, then they would be disgruntled, but that would mean that their name would be on the list, and so the second possibility also couldn't occur.

In this way, she realized that it was impossible for the list of the disgruntled to be one of the original one thousand lists.

We will use this argument to give a proof of Cantor's theorem.

Proof. We start by assuming we have been given a set S. It is clear that $|S| \leq |\mathcal{P}(S)|$. We must show that the two cardinalities cannot be equal. This will be done if we can show that it is impossible to construct a bijection $f : S \to \mathcal{P}(S)$. Our goal is to show that for any set S and any function $f : S \to \mathcal{P}(S)$, f can never be a bijection.

Given any $s \in S$, $f(s)$ will be an element of $\mathcal{P}(S)$. This means that $f(s)$ is a subset of S. There are two possibilities: either s belongs to this subset or it doesn't. We can write this as either $s \in f(s)$ or $s \notin f(s)$. (Compare s to a person and $f(s)$ to the list the person receives.)

We now define a set T by defining it to contain all the elements s of S that are not contained in their image $f(s)$. More formally we can write

$$T = \{s \in S | s \notin f(s)\}.$$

(This is the list of disgruntled people.)

The set T is a subset of S, so T is an element of $\mathcal{P}(S)$. We will now show that there cannot exist a $t \in S$ with $f(t) = T$. This will mean that T does not have a partner in S and consequently f cannot be a bijection.

We use a proof by contradiction, so we start with the assumption that there is a $t \in S$ with $f(t) = T$ and we must show that this leads to a contradiction.

We can ask whether t is an element of T. There are two possibilities: it either is or is not. We will show that both possibilities give a contradiction.

If $t \in T$, then this means that $t \in f(t) = T$. This gives a contradiction because T is defined to be exactly the elements s that are not elements of $f(s)$.

If $t \notin T$, then this means that $t \notin f(t) = T$. Since T is defined to be exactly the elements s that are not elements of $f(s)$ it follows that t must be an element of T. Again we have a contradiction.

Since our assumption that there is $t \in S$ with $f(t) = T$ gives a contradiction, it must be the case that there is no element of S that is partnered with T. Consequently, f cannot be a bijection, which shows that S and $\mathcal{P}(S)$ cannot have the same cardinality.

$\square$

The proof we have just completed is quite complicated. To illustrate what is going on we will look at the specific example where $S = \{0, 1, 2\}$ and

$$\mathcal{P}(S) = \{\{0, 1, 2\}, \{0, 1\}, \{0, 2\}, \{1, 2\}, \{0\}, \{1\}, \{2\}, \{\}\}.$$

We will choose $f : S \to \mathcal{P}(S)$ to be the function with

$$f(0) = \{0, 1, 2\}, f(1) = \{0\} \text{ and } f(2) = \{1\}.$$

For this example

$$0 \in f(0) \text{ but } 1 \notin f(1) \text{ and } 2 \notin f(2).$$

The set T is defined to be the elements $s \notin f(s)$, so $T = \{1, 2\}$. The proof shows that there is no element $t \in S$ with $f(t)$ equal to T. In our example, it is clearly seen that T is not the image of any element of S.

It is a good exercise to take different choices for f and show that the T you get for each choice is never in the image of any element of S.

The Cardinality of the Real Numbers

In this chapter we have shown that

$$|\mathbb{N}| = |\mathbb{Z}| = |\mathbb{Q}| = \aleph_0$$

and that $2^{\aleph_0} > \aleph_0$. We will now show that the cardinality of the real numbers is $2^{\aleph_0}$.

We start by looking at the real numbers that lie between 0 and 1. The notation for this is $(0, 1)$. The notation (a, b) has various meanings in mathematics, but we will always use $(0, 1)$ to denote $\{x \in \mathbb{R} | 0 < x < 1\}$.

Every real number x in $(0, 1)$ can be written as a decimal of the form

$$0.a_1 a_2 a_3 a_4 \ldots.$$

The dots indicate that the decimal expansion goes to an infinite number of places. (It is important to realize that we cannot always round off to a finite number of places, because if we do we will end up with a rational number.)

There is one small technicality when using decimals, some real numbers can have two possible decimal expansions. For example, $0.20000 \ldots$ is exactly the same number as $0.19999 \ldots$, where the 0s carry on forever in the first expression and the 9s carry on forever in the second expression. We are not saying that these numbers are very close, they are actually equal. This ambiguity only occurs with 0s and 9s. If a decimal expansion has 0s for every term after a certain point it can be rewritten as one that terminates with an infinite number of 9s. (This is only mentioned for completeness. It will not cause any problems in any of the arguments that follow.)

Consider decimal expansions of the form $0.a_1a_2a_3a_4\ldots$. We want to know how many there are. The cardinality of $(0, 1)$ is the same as the cardinality of all decimals written in this form. There are ten possibilities for the choice of a_1 (any of the digits from 0 to 9). Similarly there are ten choices for a_2, for a_3 and so on. There are an infinite number of decimal places, but we now know a little more about infinities. The infinity in this case is the cardinality of the natural numbers, $\aleph_0$, so the number of decimal expansions of the form $0.a_1a_2a_3a_4\ldots$ will be $10 \times 10 \times \cdots = 10^{\aleph_0}$, which means the cardinality of $(0, 1)$ is $10^{\aleph_0}$.

The 10 that appears in the expression comes from the fact that we are dealing with decimals. We could have made exactly the same argument using binary numbers. All real numbers in $(0, 1)$ can be written in binary form as $0.b_1b_2b_3\ldots$. This time there are only two choices for each b_i, either 0 or 1. Proceeding as before, we obtain the cardinality of $(0, 1)$ is $2^{\aleph_0}$. One of the implications of this is that $2^{\aleph_0} = 10^{\aleph_0}$. (We could have used the same argument using numbers to any base, which tells us that $2^{\aleph_0} = n^{\aleph_0}$ for any natural number $n \geq 2$.)

The astute reader might be concerned that the argument that the cardinality of $(0, 1)$ is $10^{\aleph_0}$ is not quite right. The $10^{\aleph_0}$ came from looking at all possible decimal expansions, but we have noted that sometimes two different decimal expansions correspond to the same real number. There are $\aleph_0$ real numbers with two representations (real numbers that have two representations are rational numbers), so the cardinality of $(0, 1)$ is $10^{\aleph_0} - \aleph_0$. However, $\aleph_0$ is negligible compared to the larger cardinal $10^{\aleph_0}$ and it can be shown that $10^{\aleph_0} - \aleph_0 = 10^{\aleph_0}$.

At this point you might be feeling that this proof is getting pretty complicated and wish that there was an easier proof. This was exactly the same feeling that Cantor had. He gave another, simpler proof that $|(0, 1)| > \aleph_0$. We will give this in the next section. It will also explain why these arguments are called "diagonal."

We are on our way of determining the cardinality of the reals. We have determined that the cardinality of the unit interval $(0, 1)$ is $2^{\aleph_0}$. The final step in the argument show that $(0, 1)$ has the same cardinality as the set of real numbers. We do this by constructing a bijection between them.

An example of a graph of a bijection is sketched below. It has vertical asymptotes at $x = 0$ and at $x = 1$. The y-values approach negative infinity as x approaches 0 from the right and positive infinity as x approaches 1 from the left.

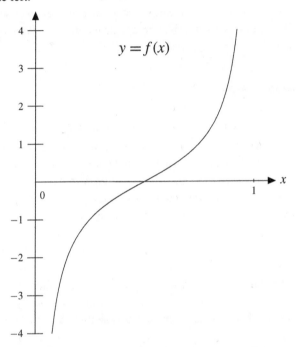

$y = f(x)$

For readers who have seen trigonometric functions and are curious, the function, $f{:}(0, 1) \rightarrow \mathbb{R}$, that is graphed is given by $f(x) = \tan((x - 0.5)\pi))$.

Once we know that there is a bijection between $(0, 1)$ and $\mathbb{R}$, we know that they have the same cardinality. Since $|(0, 1)| = 2^{\aleph_0}$, we have shown that $|\mathbb{R}| = 2^{\aleph_0}$. We now know

$$|\mathbb{N}| = |\mathbb{Z}| = |\mathbb{Q}| < |\mathbb{R}|.$$

The real numbers consist of the rational numbers and the irrational numbers. The difference in cardinality between the reals and the rationals is caused by the irrationals. The cardinality of the irrational numbers is $2^{\aleph_0}$, which is a larger infinity than that of the rationals. Consequently, though the real numbers consist of the rationals and the irrationals, they are practically all irrational. This is another surprising consequence of Cantor's work.

The proof that the cardinality of the reals is greater than the cardinality of the natural numbers is a striking result. Cantor gave another somewhat simpler proof of this result using the diagonal argument. We look at this proof next.

The Diagonal Argument

If a set has cardinality $\aleph_0$ it is called a *countable* set. This is because if $|S| = \aleph_0$ there must be a bijection between the set S and the natural numbers. Each element of S can be paired with a unique natural number. We will denote the element of S that is paired with the natural number n by s_n. Then we can describe the set S by saying $S = \{s_1, s_2, s_3, \ldots\}$. We have ordered the elements of S so that we have a first one, a second one, and so on.

If a set S has cardinality greater than $\aleph_0$ then it is called an *uncountable* set. We cannot write it in the form $\{s_1, s_2, s_3, \ldots\}$, because this only describes a countable, $\aleph_0$, number of elements and so there are infinitely many elements of S that will be missed. In fact, practically every element will be missed. A cardinal number is negligible compared to larger cardinals.

Cantor's diagonal proof is a proof that the set of real numbers in the interval $(0, 1)$ is uncountable.

Proof. It is proof by contradiction. Cantor begins by assuming that the real numbers in $(0, 1)$ are countable and derives a contradiction. We start with the assumption $(0, 1)$ is countable, so we can write the set as $\{r_1, r_2, r_3, \ldots\}$. Each of the real numbers r_i can be written as a decimal. We will use the following notation for these decimals

$$r_1 = 0.a_{11}a_{12}a_{13}\ldots, r_2 = 0.a_{21}a_{22}a_{23}\ldots, \ldots, r_i = 0.a_{i1}a_{i2}a_{i3}\ldots, \ldots.$$

Writing this in a vertical list gives:

$$r_1 = 0.\boldsymbol{a_{11}}a_{12}a_{13}\ldots a_{1i}\ldots$$
$$r_2 = 0.a_{21}\boldsymbol{a_{22}}a_{23}\ldots a_{1i}\ldots$$
$$r_3 = 0.a_{31}a_{32}\boldsymbol{a_{33}}\ldots a_{1i}\ldots$$
$$\vdots$$
$$r_i = 0.a_{i1}a_{i2}a_{i3}\ldots \boldsymbol{a_{ii}}\ldots$$
$$\vdots$$

Now construct a real number $b = 0.b_1b_2b_3\ldots b_i\ldots$ in the following way. Choose b_1 to be 4 unless $a_{11} = 4$ in which case let $b_1 = 5$. Choose b_2 to be 4 unless $a_{22} = 4$ in which case let $b_2 = 5$. In general, choose b_i to be 4 unless $a_{ii} = 4$ in which case let $b_i = 5$. We are looking at the diagonal elements in the list and choosing b_i to differ from the ith diagonal digit.

First note that the decimal expansion of b only involves the digits 4 and 5, so b is not a real number that can have two decimal expansions (the ambiguous ones involve 0s and 9s). Also note that b is a real number in the interval $(0, 1)$. Since b is a real number in $(0, 1)$ it must, by hypothesis, be on the list.

However, since b_1 is not equal to a_{11}, we know that $b \neq r_1$. Since b_2 is not equal to a_{22}, we know that $b \neq r_2$. In general, since b_i is not equal to a_{ii} we know that $b \neq r_i$. This argument shows that b cannot be on the list.

We have shown that b is both on the list and also not on the list. We have derived a contradiction. Consequently, the initial hypothesis must be wrong and the real numbers contained in $(0, 1)$ are not countable. $\square$

The Continuum Hypothesis

Cantor had shown that $\aleph_0$ was less than $2^{\aleph_0}$, that the cardinality of the natural numbers was less than the cardinality of the reals. He considered the obvious question of whether there was a cardinal number that lies strictly between $\aleph_0$ and $2^{\aleph_0}$ or, equivalently, whether there is some subset of the real numbers that has cardinality greater than $\aleph_0$ but less than $2^{\aleph_0}$. He didn't believe that there was, but was unable to prove it. The hypothesis that there is no cardinal number between $\aleph_0$ and $2^{\aleph_0}$ became known as the *continuum hypothesis*.

Hilbert, in 1900, listed twenty three problems that he considered the most important for the new century. The first of these was the continuum hypothesis.

In 1940, Gödel showed that the continuum hypothesis could not be disproven from the axioms of set theory. In 1963, Paul Cohen showed that it was not possible to prove the continuum hypothesis from the axioms. This showed that the continuum hypothesis is independent of the axioms — a statement that can neither be proved or disproved from them.

The Cardinality of Computations

We return our attention to machines and computations to see what we can say about the cardinality of all possible computations that can be done by a computer.

First we will look at computations that can be done by finite automata. A computation consists of a finite automaton and a finite input. Since we can design infinitely many finite automata and give them infinitely many inputs, there must be an infinite number of computations that can be done by finite automata. This means that the cardinality of the number of computations is at least $\aleph_0$.

In the section on encodings we showed how, given any finite automaton M and a finite input string I, we could encode both pieces of information in $\langle M, I \rangle$. This encoding was a string of 0s and 1s that always began with four 1s. An example we looked at had

$$\langle M, I \rangle = 1111001110111001011010011111110010110.$$

There is no reason why we cannot consider the string as being a number. If we add commas in the appropriate places $\langle M, I \rangle$ can be considered as the rather large number

$$111,100,111,011,100,101,101,001,111,110,010,110.$$

Thought of in this way, encodings give a function from finite automata and finite inputs to the natural numbers. A computation done by a finite automaton consists of the automaton and a finite input. We now have a function from computations to the natural numbers. Distinct computations get sent to distinct natural numbers. This means that there is a bijection between the set of computations and a subset of the natural numbers. Consequently the cardinality of the set of computations that can be done by finite automata is at most $\aleph_0$.

We have shown that the cardinality of computations that can be done by finite automata is at most $\aleph_0$ and at least $\aleph_0$. The conclusion is that the set of all possible computations done by finite automata has cardinality $\aleph_0$. Though they can perform infinitely many computations they can perform only countably many.

The entire argument that we have just made for finite automata can be extended to Turing machines and their calculations. Given a Turing machine and an input string, we can encode the information and think of this string as a natural number. The conclusion of the argument is the same. The set of all possible computations done by Turing machines has cardinality $\aleph_0$. Though they can perform infinitely many computations they can perform only countably many.

Any computation done by a computer can also be done by a Turing machine, so only countably many computations can be done by computers.

Computable Numbers

The first line in Turing's 1936 paper is "The 'computable numbers' may be described briefly as the real numbers whose expressions as decimal are calculable by finite means." This is the beginning of the paper and so he hasn't defined the idea of a Turing machine yet, but what he means by 'finite means' is by a Turing machine or algorithm.

A computable number is a real number for which there was a Turing machine and an input and, when the machine runs on the input, it prints out the decimal expansion of the number on the tape. However, Turing was not interested in just finite decimal expansions, which would restrict computable numbers to the rationals. He wanted the machine's output to include irrationals. He did this by describing machines that were different from the ones that we have described. Turing's machines didn't have accept and reject states, and they could run forever. To print out an irrational number he allowed the machine to keep running as long as it kept printing out the appropriate digits.

Nowadays, we define Turing machines in the way that we have in this book. Our machines must always halt in an accept state to complete a computation. When a computation is accepted there can only be a finite number of symbols on the tape. We need a trick to be able to deal with infinite decimal expansions.

We define a real number c to be computable if there exists a Turing machine (or algorithm, if you prefer) that takes as input any natural number n and after a finite number of steps halts with the decimal expansion of the number c correct to n decimal places. In this way the computation always halts, but by inputting the number n, we can get the answer as accurate as we like.

Turing showed that all rational numbers were computable. He showed that irrational numbers that often crop up in mathematics like $\sqrt{2}$, π and e were all computable. In fact, it is quite likely that you have never come across a number that is not computable. We will show that practically all real numbers are not computable, so we really ought to have a concrete example of one of these numbers.

A Non-Computable Number

In the previous chapter we showed that the maximum shifts function, $S(n)$, was not a computable function. We will use this to construct our non-computable number.

We will define a number N so that $0 < N < 1$. The decimal expansion of N will consist entirely of 0s and 1s. The position of the 1s will be given by $S(n)$. Formally, we define

$$N = \sum_{n=1}^{\infty} \frac{1}{10^{S(n)}}.$$

Recall that $S(1) = 1$, $S(2) = 6$ and $S(3) = 21$. Consequently,

$$N = \frac{1}{10^1} + \frac{1}{10^6} + \frac{1}{10^{21}} + \cdots = 0.100001000000000000001000\ldots$$

with the next 1 occurring at the 107th decimal place ($S(4) = 107$).

If we could compute N, then we could compute the positions of the 1s in its decimal expansion and then we could compute $S(n)$. However, we have shown that $S(n)$ is not a computable function. This means that N cannot be a computable number.

The number N is perfectly well-defined, even though it is not computable. The fact that there exist numbers that you can define but not compute is an interesting consequence of Turing's work.

It might seem that non-computable numbers are fairly exotic and rare, but this is far from being true. We will show that computable numbers are countable, which means that the practically all real numbers are non-computable.

There Is a Countable Number of Computable Numbers

We will let $\mathbb{K}$ denote the computable numbers. Since $\mathbb{K}$ contains $\mathbb{Q}$ and we know that the cardinality of the rationals is $\aleph_0$, we can deduce that

$$\aleph_0 \leq |\mathbb{K}|.$$

We also know that the set of all possible computations that can be done by Turing machines is $\aleph_0$, and that the set of computable numbers is a subset of all possible computations, so we have

$$|\mathbb{K}| \leq \aleph_0.$$

The two inequalities tell us that the set of computable numbers is countable.

$$|\mathbb{K}| = \aleph_0.$$

Computable Numbers Are Not Effectively Enumerable

We have seen that the computable numbers are countable. Consequently, there exists a bijection between them and the natural numbers. Turing showed that though there must be a bijection, this bijection cannot be found by an Turing machine. There is no algorithm, or effective procedure, that will list the computable numbers. This is what is meant by saying that the computable numbers are not *effectively enumerable*.

We will just consider the computable numbers that are larger than 0 and less than 1 and give Turing's proof for this set. This subset of the computable numbers is countable. Again, this means that there is a bijection between them and the natural numbers. As we noted before, we can use this bijection to list these computable numbers as $\{c_1, c_2, c_3, \dots\}$ where c_1 is the countable number paired with 1, c_2 the one paired with 2 and so on. We can now perform Cantor's diagonal argument. First we list the decimal expansions:

$$c_1 = 0.\mathbf{a_{11}}a_{12}a_{13}\dots a_{1i}\dots$$
$$c_2 = 0.a_{21}\mathbf{a_{22}}a_{23}\dots a_{2i}\dots$$
$$c_3 = 0.a_{31}a_{32}\mathbf{a_{33}}\dots a_{3i}\dots$$
$$\vdots$$
$$c_i = 0.a_{i1}a_{i2}a_{i3}\dots \mathbf{a_{ii}}\dots$$
$$\vdots$$

As before we can construct a real number $b = 0.b_1 b_2 b_3 \dots b_i \dots$ in exactly the same way. Choose b_1 to be 4 unless $a_{11} = 4$ in which case let $b_1 = 5$. Choose b_2 to be 4 unless $a_{22} = 4$ in which case let $b_2 = 5$. In general, choose b_i to be 4 unless $a_{ii} = 4$ in which case let $b_i = 5$. We are looking at the diagonal elements in the list and choosing b_i to differ from the ith diagonal digit.

As we noted before, the number b is a real number that lies between 0 and 1 and it cannot be on the list. The list contains all the computable numbers. This must mean that b is not a computable number. But why not? The process of constructing b from the list can be described by an algorithm: Go to first element in the list, look at the digit in the first decimal place. If it is not 4, print 4. If it is 4, print 5. Now repeat the process with the second element, looking at the second decimal place — and so on. However, we know that b is not on the list of computable numbers. The only conclusion is that the list of computable numbers is not something that can be constructed by a computer. If the list could be constructed by a computer, then *b* would be computable and we would have a contradiction. If it is not possible to construct the list by a computer, then there is no contradiction, so that must be the case.

The title of Turing's paper is "On Computable Numbers, with An application to the Entscheidungsproblem." This title should now make sense. Turing wanted to show that Hilbert's view of the Entscheidungsproblem was not correct. To recap: He first needed to give a definition of an effective procedure, or algorithm. This he did through his definition of what we now call Turing machines. Then Turing needed to find a problem that could not be answered by an algorithm. He defined the computable numbers and showed that they were countable. Then he proved that there was no algorithm that could list these numbers, by showing that if there were such an algorithm, we could use it to compute the diagonal number, which is not on the list. But this would contradict the list including all possible computable numbers.

Turing had proved one of the greatest mathematicians wrong. It was an important result. However, the real genius was in the method. His theoretical machines that were simple to understand and yet, as he showed, were capable of doing any computation. His argument showed the existence of the universal computer and then showed its power and its limits.

The paper now stands as the foundation of theoretical computer science.

9 Turing's Legacy

"Can submarines swim?"
Edsger W. Dijkstra[1]

We have looked at the ideas contained in Turing's 1936 paper and commented that the paper now stands as the foundation of computer science. But when Turing wrote the paper, it was a result in mathematical logic, computer science did not yet exist as an academic discipline, and the modern computer had not been invented. In this chapter we will look at some of the history of the subsequent years. In particular, we will look at what happened after the 1936 paper was published up to Turing's death in 1954.

But first, we briefly mention Max Newman. When looking at the work of influential thinkers it is easy to underestimate the role that others played in their work. Having an active, supportive mentor can make all the difference, and Newman played this role for Turing throughout his professional life.

Newman was also a fellow at King's College, Cambridge while Turing was there. It was Newman who taught the course on Gödel's Incompleteness Theorem that Turing attended during the spring of 1935, and it was in this course that Turing first learned of the Entscheidungsproblem. It was Newman, a year later, who realized that Turing's approach to computation was both highly original and important, and encouraged him to submit his paper for publication. Newman also wrote to the editor of the *London Mathematical Society* explaining what Turing had done and urged him to accept Turing's paper for publication.

During the war both Turing and Newman worked at Bletchley Park on code breaking. After the war, Newman would go on to found the Royal Society Computing Machine Laboratory at the University of Manchester, and would invite Turing to join this group. Turing would work at Manchester from 1948 until his death in 1954.

Newman also helped Turing to make the decision to go to Princeton and work with Alonzo Church.

Turing at Princeton

Princeton, in New Jersey, houses both Princeton University and the Institute for Advanced Study. In 1936, both the Princeton University Mathematics Department and the Institute were housed in the same building, the original Fine Hall — now renamed Jones Hall. Alonzo Church was a professor at the university, Albert Einstein and John von Neumann were members of the Institute. Kurt Gödel had visited the Institute in 1934 and in 1935, and would become a permanent member in 1939. It was a major center for mathematics and in particular for mathematical logic.

In 1936, Church was thirty three years old and already a well-established logician. Both Kleene and Rosser had been Church's students and both had major results in mathematical logic. Turing was just twenty four and was just starting his mathematical career. There was nobody at Cambridge that he could work with. It made sense for him to visit Church in Princeton.

Turing did not have a Ph.D. At this time it was not a requirement for academics in England, so Turing didn't need to obtain one. However, in consultation with Newman and Church, he decided that studying for a Ph.D. would provide a good reason for traveling to Princeton and for working with Church. Turing left for Princeton in September, 1936.

While at Princeton, Turing got to know von Neumann. In 1937, von Neumann wrote a letter in support of Turing's application for a fellowship. In this letter he says of Turing: "He has done good work in branches of mathematics in which I am interested, namely: theory of almost periodic functions, and theory of continuous groups."[2] There is no mention of Turing's work on computation, and it seems likely that von Neumann was not aware of Turing's *Computable Numbers* paper at this time. However, he must have learned of it shortly after. Stanisław Ulam remembers talking about Turing's work with von Neumann in the summer of 1938 and also during the following year, writing, "... von Neumann mentioned to me Turing's name several times in 1939 in conversations, concerning mechanical ways to develop formal mathematical systems."[3]

In 1938, Turing was awarded his Ph.D. for a dissertation in which he introduced the study of ordinal logic.[4] As part of this this he invented the idea of an *oracle* — a black box that can immediately answer a question. It could be an undecidable question. We don't ask how it knows the answer. We just assume it knows. An oracle machine is a Turing machine that is connected to an oracle. Turing only introduced the idea of an oracle. It was not a major part of his dissertation and he never studied them in detail. (It would be Post who followed up and proved the major results concerning oracles in the 1940s.) But these machines have also proved to be an important part of theoretical computer science. As Robert Soare has commented, you can think of your laptop being a Turing machine and the oracle as being the web.

After Turing completed his Ph.D., von Neumann offered him a position as his assistant, but Turing decided not to accept and instead returned to England.

During the time that Turing was working on his Ph.D. another breakthrough paper was written. This was on logic and switching circuits and was written by Claude Shannon.

Claude Shannon

In 1936, Claude Shannon graduated from the University of Michigan with two undergraduate degrees; one in electrical engineering and one in mathematics. He then went to M.I.T. for graduate school. At M.I.T. he worked on an early analog computer. This work led him to consider switches and digital computing.

Switches have the property that they are either on or off. It is clear that they can represent 0 or 1, but Shannon showed they could do much more; that all of Boolean algebra and binary arithmetic could be done using electrical circuits and switches. These results became part of his master's degree thesis in 1937 and were published a year later.[5]

This paper is one of the foundational papers in the design of computers. It very quickly became widely known among electrical engineers and influenced the design of all subsequent digital computers.

Second World War

After his time at Princeton, Turing returned to his position at Cambridge, but also started working on code breaking for the Government Code and Cipher School (GC&CS).[6] When Britain declared war on Germany in September 1939, Turing moved to Bletchley Park, the wartime location of GC&CS, to work full time on cryptanalysis.

Germany was using Enigma machines to encode and decode all of their military's messages. These machines had a keyboard in which the operator typed letters. Their interiors contained a number of rotors. At the start of the encoding process, the operator had to insert the rotors in a certain order, then rotate them to the appropriate initial setting. There were also plugboards that had to be wired as part of the initial configuration.

Once the machine was configured, the operator typed the message. As each letter was typed the rotors rotated and the encrypted version of the letter was shown via an illuminated display, which the operator wrote down. After the operator had encoded the entire message, he transmitted it to the receiver using standard Morse code.

The coding had a self-inverse property, in that the receiver would set his machine to exactly the same agreed upon starting configuration and type the encrypted message. Again, as each letter was typed, he would write down the letter shown in the illuminated display. At the end of the process he would have the original plaintext message written down.

Breaking this code required two steps. The first was to understand exactly how the Enigma was constructed. How did the rotors change the encoding as each letter was typed? What was the wiring between rotors? How did the wiring of the plugboard work? After it was known exactly how the encoding process worked, the second step was to discover the initial settings of the machine for each intercepted message.

Before the war had started, the Poles had completed both steps. The Polish mathematician Marian Rejewski and his team of cryptologists had managed to reverse engineer the Enigma machine and had worked out the complete wiring diagram. This was a remarkable feat that required knowledge about abstract properties of permutations. Statistics and probability had always been in the cryptologists' toolbox, but Rejewski realized that theorems in an area of pure mathematics called *group theory* could help in determining how the machine worked. His group theoretic methods were stunningly successful.

The Polish cryptologists also discovered a weakness in the way that the initial settings were sent at the start of a message. This error on Germany's part meant that it was possible to determine the initial rotor settings from just the first six letters of the encrypted message. It was just a question of searching through a table of all possible six letter sequences that could be generated by all possible orderings of the rotors, all possible rotor settings and all possible plugboard wirings. The problem was that this number of possibilities is enormous. At the start of the war there were about 10^{22} possible initial settings for the machine (later they added rotors and the number of initial settings increased even further). To give some idea of the enormity of this number, if you could examine a million settings each second, it would still take one hundred million years to run through them all.

Rejewski and his team approached the problem in two ways. They realized they needed to use group theoretical ideas to limit the number of possibilities that needed to be checked, and they needed a machine that would look through this restricted list. They constructed a machine, the *bomba kryptologiczna*, to do the search. The essence of their machine was six Enigmas wired together in such a way that they worked together in searching through the restricted list of possible settings until a match was found.

By 1938, Poland could decode the majority of military messages that they intercepted. The British became aware of what the Polish cryptologists had achieved just before Germany invaded Poland in September 1939. The Poles invited British cryptologists to Warsaw where they explained everything.

However, Germany gradually made their encodings more secure. The machines still used three rotors, but there were now five possible rotors that could be installed in any of the three positions. The transmission of the initial settings was changed to eliminate the weakness that the Poles had been exploiting. These changes happened at different times for different parts of military, but the navy was a priority. Being able to decrypt messages that would provide locations of German submarines and ships would give the Allies a tremendous strategic advantage, and consequently the German cryptologists made sure that the Naval enigma was the most secure. It wasn't long before Rejewski's methods were no longer powerful enough to decrypt them.

This is where Turing came in. He worked on encoded messages from the German navy. Turing exploited another weakness in the German system. This was that every letter had to be encrypted as a different letter; no letter could be encrypted as itself. Consequently, if you had a phrase that you were fairly sure was in the message, you could slide the letters of the phrase above letters in the encoded message until you found a place where no letters matched. This sequence of letters was then a possible encoding of your phrase. This idea, along with ideas from group theory and probability theory enabled him, like Rejewski, to design a machine containing multiple copies of Enigmas wired together in such a way that they performed the search through a restricted set of possibilities. His first *bombe* was operational in the spring of 1940.[7]

In 1942, after the United States joined the war, Turing went to America to work with cryptologists there, helping with the design of American bombes. While in America, he visited Bell Labs, which was then in lower Manhattan, where he met Claude Shannon. In addition to working on cryptology, they discussed their work on computing.[8]

At the end of the war there were a large number of bombes working in both the US and England. Being able to read Germany's messages enabled the allies to locate German U-boats and the routes of ships. It helped with the choice of when and where to attack.

Turing and Rejewski had not only played an important part in winning the war, but had ushered cryptology into a new age. From this time forward, it would be based on sophisticated mathematics and it would require large amounts of computation.

Max Newman was also at Bletchley during the war. He spearheaded the effort to break another German encryption machine that the English called *Tunny*. Tunny was a much more sophisticated encryption method than the Enigma. It was designed for the High Command in Germany to send messages to the front-line generals. Newman needed something more powerful than the bombes to break these codes. He was introduced to Tommy Flowers by Turing. Flowers was an expert in the use of vacuum tubes.[9] He proposed and then built a large scale electronic machine to attack Tunny. Up to this point vacuum tubes had been considered too unreliable to use in large numbers in one machine, but Flowers showed that the common wisdom was wrong. His machine, called the *Colossus*, was reliable, fast and powerful. It showed that the future of computation would be with electronic machines as opposed to electromechanical machines.

At the end of the war there were eleven of these machines. Two of the machines were kept for code breaking, but the other nine along with all of their documentation, deemed possible security risks, were destroyed.[10]

In 1945, Turing was awarded the OBE[11] by King George VI for his work in cryptology. Newman felt that Turing deserved more recognition for his wartime work, and when, six months later, he was also offered the OBE, he declined it in protest.

Though the specific design of the Colossus was to be kept secret, the knowledge that computing machines could be constructed was fairly widely known. Several groups in different parts of the world were now designing the first computers.

Their work done at Bletchley, both Newman and Turing left to work on the design and construction of new machines. Newman, salvaging a few parts from a dismantled Colossus, moved to Manchester University to set up the Computing Machine Laboratory; Turing went to the National Physical Laboratory in London to design his own machine.

Development of Computers in the 1940s

During the 1940s computers evolved from sophisticated programmable calculating machines to essentially modern computers. The major steps along the way were: designing machines to be universal computers rather than machines specialized for certain types of computation; the switch from electromechanical devices to electronic ones; and finally the stored-program computer in which both the program and data can be read into memory.

The answer to who built the first computer really depends on your definition of computer. Most people would agree that the definition should include that the machine be universal. It also seems reasonable that you should include the fact that the machine is not theoretically universal, but designed to be universal in practice. For example, Konrad Zuse built a machine called the Z3 in 1941. It was designed for specific calculations. It was not designed to be universal, but in 1998 it was proved that by manipulating the input in certain ways that it could, in fact, do any computation. On the other hand, Zuse's Z4 was designed to be a general purpose computer.

Instead of trying to give the credit to one person, it seems to make more sense to outline some of the major steps along the way to the modern stored-program electronic computer.

Konrad Zuse

The Second World War provided a major impetus for constructing computing machines — problems involving not only codes, but also ballistic tables and weapon design needed massive amounts of computation that could no longer be feasibly handled solely by human computers. Both the Allied and Axis powers began to design machines to do these computations. For the Axis powers, the German engineer, Konrad Zuse, built a series of sophisticated and innovative electromechanical machines. Zuse was not aware of either of Shannon's or Turing's work and worked entirely independently. His Z4 built in 1945 is the first universal computer that was designed to be universal. (As noted above his Z3 which has been proved to be universal, but was not designed to be universal.) The Z4 became operational during the last days of the war in Berlin. As the allied bombing on Berlin intensified, the machine was packed up and sent to Göttingen. It was some time before Zuse continued his work on it, but in 1950 a working version was again running.

Mauchly and Eckert

The next step towards constructing the modern computer was the shift from electromechanical devices to electrical ones — the shift from relays to vacuum tubes. The first universal, electronic computer was ENIAC, containing 17468 vacuum tubes. This was built by John Mauchly and J. Presper Eckert at the University of Pennsylvania. They started work in 1943 and the machine was fully functional in 1946. However, it was not a stored-program computer in which both the data and program are stored in memory. Programming ENIAC required plugging in various wires and setting switches.

Von Neumann

Von Neumann was interested in the intellectual problems involved in the design of computers, but he also needed a computer to be actually built. He was involved in the construction of the first hydrogen bomb and this needed massive calculations. These calculations simulated the effects of the shockwaves, first from the conventional explosives that detonated the fissionable material, then from the fission explosion that was needed to detonate the fusion reaction. Careful design was needed so that the bomb would actually reach the fusion stage without blowing itself to pieces at an earlier stage. Since it was clearly not practical to keep testing actual bombs with different designs, it was decided that the testing would be done by simulating chain reactions on machines.

Von Neumann worked closely with Mauchly and Eckert as they built ENIAC. Together, with a few others, they looked at how the design could be improved for the next generation of computers. Von Neumann stressed the stored-program concept — that the program should be stored in exactly the same way as the data.

The "First Draft of a Report on the EDVAC" was a summary of the ideas of the joint group. Herman Goldstine, who was also part of the group, typed up von Neumann's notes to produce the paper. These notes originally contained gaps where von Neumann was going to insert references, but both the gaps and references were omitted in the typed copy. Goldstine also gave the report its title, *First Draft of a Report on the EDVAC*, and credited it solely to von Neumann. After typing it, he mimeographed twenty-four copies and distributed them. The paper was widely circulated in 1945 and influenced the design of subsequent computers. This design for a stored-program, electronic computer has since become known as the von Neumann architecture.

Mauchly and Eckert were extremely upset that they were not listed as co-authors. Not only did von Neumann seem to be taking credit for many ideas that they thought belonged to them, but he had also put them into the public domain. They were planning on patenting their ideas and licensing them. Now they were in the public domain, that would not be possible.[12] Turing's name was also missing from the report, but despite the lack of reference, the stored-program idea is essentially his. As Stanley Frankel wrote:

... in about 1943 or '44 von Neumann was well aware of the fundamental importance of Turing's paper ... . Von Neumann introduced me to that paper and at his urging I studied it with care ... he firmly emphasized to me, and to others I am sure, that the fundamental conception is owing to Turing — in so far as not anticipated by Babbage, Lovelace and others.[13]

Turing needed the fact that programs can be encoded as strings of numbers for his diagonalization argument, but understanding that we can think of these strings of numbers in two ways — as numbers and as programs — is one of the important ideas in the design of computers. It is this that enables us to treat programs as data. For example, this is what enables us to construct high level languages, where the program is compiled by a compiler that regards the program as data; this is what enables us to form computer networks. As George Dyson writes, "The stored-program computer, as conceived by Alan Turing and delivered by John von Neumann, broke the distinction between numbers that *mean* things and numbers that *do* things. Our universe would never be the same."[14]

After the circulation of von Neumann's *Draft*, there was a race on to build the first stored-program computer. The Manchester Small-Scale Experimental machine, also known as *the baby*, was the first, in 1948. Newman was the director of the laboratory and Turing joined that year. However, the *baby* and the later *Manchester Mark 1* were built by Frederic Williams and Tom Kilburn; neither Turing nor Newman had a major role in their design or construction. The *baby* was designed as a prototype to test the first random-access storage device which was going to be part of the full-scale computer, the *Mark 1*.

Several different groups built and had running full-scale universal, electronic, stored-program computers in 1949. The *Mark 1* in

Manchester and the *EDSAC* at Cambridge University were running within a month of one another. A few months later *CSIRAC* built in Sydney, Australia was up and running. Ironically, all of these were based on von Neumann's *First Draft of a Report on the EDVAC*, but the *EDVAC* wasn't operational until 1951.

The Turing Test

Immediately after the war Turing went to work at the National Physical Laboratory in London. While there, he decided to design his own computer. He named it the Automatic Computing Engine (ACE) and produced a complete design of the machine. A small group started work on building the ACE, but work progressed slowly. A prototype was eventually up and running in 1950, but by this time there were other more powerful computers, and even Turing had decamped to Newman's group at Manchester University, where he would work until his death.

While at Manchester, Turing published a paper called *Computing Machinery and Intelligence*. The paper starts with the question "Can machines think?" Turing considers how we can tell whether a person or a machine is thinking. He proposes the *Imitation Game*, which has since become known as the "Turing Test." In this game a human interrogator is in a separate room from a computer and another human. The interrogator knows the computer and human as *A* and *B*, but does not know which is which. The interrogator asks *A* and *B* questions which they answer. The goal is for the interrogator to determine which of *A* or *B* is the human and which is the computer.[15]

Like *Computable Numbers*, this is a very interesting paper, but unlike *Computable Numbers*, it is also an easy paper to read. (It is available on the web and is well worth reading.) Turing writes eloquently and considers various objections to the idea that machines can think. He is highly original. One of his concerns is that the humans might be able to communicate telepathically, a problem that he takes quite seriously, suggesting that everyone be put in "telepathy-proof" rooms.

Turing's central thesis is that we tell if someone is conscious and is thinking by interacting with the person. We don't try to understand how their brains are working in terms of neurons, but see if we can have a meaningful dialog. The same should be true of machines. If we want to know whether a machine is intelligent or conscious, we should do this by interaction, not by dissection.

It is interesting to note that nowadays there is a version of the Turing test that has become part of our everyday lives. Only in this version it is the computer that is trying to distinguish between humans and machines. CAPTCHAs (for Completely Automated Public Turing Test To Tell Computers and Humans Apart) often appear in online forms. Before you can submit the form, you have to answer a CAPTCHA, which customarily involves reading some deformed text and typing the letters and numbers into a box.

The notion of machines thinking naturally leads to the notions of whether machines can understand and can be conscious. There have been heated arguments both for and against. The most famous argument against the idea of machines as entities that can think and understand is the *Chinese Room Argument*.

This is a thought experiment invented by the philosopher John Searle in 1980, and is based on the Turing Test. Searle imagines that he has been placed in a room. He doesn't understand a word of Chinese, but he has a book that tells him what to do in various situations. People can slide pieces of paper into the room through a slot. Searle can write on pieces of paper and slide them back through the slot to the people on the outside. The people on the outside are native speakers of Chinese. On the pieces of paper they are writing questions in Chinese. Searle looks at the message. It is meaningless to him, but he can look up the strings of symbols in his book. When he finds the appropriate string it tells him what to write on his piece of paper and slide to the people outside.

The people on the outside are Chinese interrogators. They are trying to determine whether there is someone or something inside the room who understands Chinese. Since they keep getting correct responses to their questions they assume that there is. Does the Chinese room *understand* Chinese or is it just *simulating understanding* Chinese?

Ever since the argument was first given, it has provoked an enormous number of arguments both for and against whether real understanding is taking place. Clearly, Searle is acting as a universal computer and the book is the program. We saw that universal computers can be very simple and that the hard work goes into writing the program. Searle plus the book "thinks" exactly like a computer with a program "thinks."

The quote at the start of the chapter about submarines swimming illustrates the problems about machines 'thinking.' What does thinking entail? What does it mean to be 'conscious?' These are hard problems. Philosophers are not sure what it means for humans to be conscious, some even believe that our sense of free will is illusory and that our sense of being conscious is just an epiphenomenon of a physical brain.

Trying to explicitly define the difference, if any, between understanding and simulating understanding seems beyond us. Scott Aaronson, the M.I.T. computer scientist, sums up things nicely by saying

One can indeed give weighty and compelling arguments against the possibility of thinking machines. The only problem with these arguments is that they're also arguments against the possibility of thinking *brains*!

So, for example: one popular argument is that, if a computer appears to be intelligent, that's merely a reflection of the intelligence of the humans who programmed it. But what if humans' intelligence is just a reflection of the billion-year evolutionary process that gave rise to it? [16]

Downfall

Turing was homosexual at a time when male homosexual sex was illegal in England. In 1952, his house was broken into and Turing reported the break-in to the police. During the course of the investigation it became clear to the police that Turing was sexually involved with a man, Arnold Murray, who was connected to the burglary. Turing admitted to having had sex with Murray on three occasions. This amounted to the admission of six crimes. Three of commission of an act of gross indecency and three of being party to an act of gross indecency. The police decided to prosecute both Turing and Murray.

Turing was very worried about serving a prison term. At the trial, his defense suggested that instead of prison, Turing should receive hormone treatment and be put on probation. The judge agreed, sentencing Turing to a year's probation and ordering him to submit to organo-therapy.

(Organo-therapy is often called chemical castration and consists of receiving synthetic estrogen.)

After his conviction, Turing lost his security clearance and could no longer consult with GCHQ on questions connected to code breaking, but he still had his position at the Computing Machine Laboratory in Manchester and he continued his research. However, two years later, in June 1954, Turing was found dead of cyanide poisoning.

The widely circulated story is that Turing committed suicide by eating an apple dipped in a solution of cyanide. The philosopher and Director of the Turing Archive for the History of Computing, B. Jack Copeland, in his book *Turing: Pioneer of the Information Age* has carefully studied the events surrounding his death and concludes that while the story might be true, there is not much evidence for it. There seems to be at least as much evidence pointing towards an accidental death.

Turing was discovered by his house-cleaner. There was a half-eaten apple near the body, but apparently it was not uncommon for Turing to leave half-eaten apples lying about. The apple in question was never tested. The police investigating his death did find electrolysis equipment, a pan with liquid connected to electrodes. The equipment was still running when the police found it. The liquid was bubbling.

Turing liked to perform chemical experiments and some of these involved cyanide. He had a small room off his bedroom that he used as his laboratory. He had successfully gold-plated a spoon using electrolysis. This was a process in which the gold had been dissolved in a cyanide solution. Given these facts, it does seem possible that Turing's death could have been caused by some accidental mistake made while conducting a dangerous experiment involving cyanide.

Copeland also looks into Turing's state of mind during the last few days before his death. He notes that the hormone treatments had ceased over a year before. His work was going well. People who interacted with him during the last week of his life thought he was in good spirits and not depressed, and that he did not give any appearance of being suicidal.

The inquest into the death was very cursory. The coroner was quoted as saying "I am forced to the conclusion that this was a deliberate act. In a man of his type, one never knows what his mental processes are going to do next."[17] There seemed to be a presumption of suicide and no real examination of other possibilities.

Copeland ends his book with the words:

The exact circumstances of Turing's death may always remain unclear. It should not be stated that he committed suicide — because we just do not know. Perhaps we should just shrug our shoulders, agree that the jury is out, and focus on Turing's life and extraordinary work.

Apology and Pardon

Though we cannot be certain about the details concerning his death, it is clear that he was treated by the British justice system in a dehumanizing and barbaric way. In September, 2009, seventy years after the start of the Second World War, British Prime Minister Gordon Brown formally apologized for the way Turing was treated.

This has been a year of deep reflection — a chance for Britain, as a nation, to commemorate the profound debts we owe to those who came before. A unique combination of anniversaries and events have stirred in us that sense of pride and gratitude that characterise the British experience. Earlier this year, I stood with Presidents Sarkozy and Obama to honour the service and the sacrifice of the heroes who stormed the beaches of Normandy 65 years ago. And just last week, we marked the 70 years which have passed since the British government declared its willingness to take up arms against fascism and declared the outbreak of the Second World War. So I am both pleased and proud that thanks to a coalition of computer scientists, historians and LGBT (lesbian, gay, bisexual and transgender) activists, we have this year a chance to mark and celebrate another contribution to Britain's fight against the darkness of dictatorship: that of codebreaker Alan Turing.

Turing was a quite brilliant mathematician, most famous for his work on the German Enigma codes. It is no exaggeration to say that, without his outstanding contribution, the history of the Second World War could have been very different. He truly was one of those individuals we can point to whose unique contribution helped to turn the tide of war. The debt of gratitude he is owed makes it all the more horrifying, therefore, that he was treated so inhumanely.

In 1952, he was convicted of "gross indecency" — in effect, tried for being gay. His sentence — and he was faced with the miserable choice of this or prison — was chemical castration by a series of injections of female hormones. He took his own life just two years later.

Thousands of people have come together to demand justice for Alan Turing and recognition of the appalling way he was treated. While Turing was dealt with under the law of the time, and we can't put the clock back, his treatment was of course utterly unfair, and I am pleased to have the chance to say how deeply sorry I am and we all are for what happened to him. Alan and so many thousands of other gay men who were convicted, as he was convicted, under homophobic laws, were treated terribly. Over the years, millions more lived in fear of conviction. I am proud that those days are gone and that in the past 12 years this Government has done so much to make life fairer and more equal for our LGBT community. This recognition of Alan's status as one of Britain's most famous victims of homophobia is another step towards equality, and long overdue.

But even more than that, Alan deserves recognition for this contribution to humankind. For those of us born after 1945, into a Europe which is united, democratic and at peace, it is hard to imagine that our continent was once the theatre of mankind's darkest hour. It is difficult to believe that in living memory, people could become so consumed by hate — by anti-Semitism, by homophobia, by xenophobia and other murderous prejudices — that the gas chambers and crematoria became a piece of the European landscape as surely as the galleries and universities and concert halls which had marked out European civilisation for hundreds of years.

It is thanks to men and women who were totally committed to fighting fascism, people like Alan Turing, that the horrors of the Holocaust and of total war are part of Europe's history and not Europe's present, so on behalf of the British government, and all those who live freely thanks to Alan's work, I am very proud to say: we're sorry. You deserved so much better.

On December 24, 2013 Turing received a royal pardon.

Further Reading

Turing's papers

This book has focused on Turing's *Computable Numbers*. However, this paper is quite difficult to read as Turing was writing for an academic audience. To study it in depth, I recommend reading Charles Petzold's *The Annotated Turing: A Guided Tour Through Alan Turing's Historic Paper on Computability and the Turing Machine*. In this, Petzold takes Turing's paper and adds many excellent and lengthy annotations to help the reader understand exactly what Turing is saying at each stage. Petzold also includes the history that surrounds the paper.

The paper in which Turing discusses the Imitation Game (Turing Test) is *Computing Machinery and Intelligence*. This paper was written for a general audience and is widely available on the web. It is well worth reading.

For the reader who wants to study more of Turing's writings, Andrew Hodges maintains a website at http://www.turing.co.uk containing a wealth of information. Another online resource is the Turing Archive, maintained by Jack Copeland and Diane Proudfoot, at http://www.alanturing.net.

Biographies of Turing

A number of people have written biographies of Turing including his mother and brother. However, two biographies stand out: *Alan Turing: The Enigma* by Andrew Hodges, and *Turing: Pioneer of the Information Age* by B. Jack Copeland. Hodges's book is the more comprehensive by far, but both books are written by academic authors who really understand Turing's ideas and can explain them well.

History of the theory of computing

The Universal Computer: The Road from Leibniz to Turing by Martin Davis contains biographies and explanations of the mathematics and logic that lead up to the Turing machine.

George Dyson's *Turing's Cathedral* continues from where Davis ends, telling the story of how computers came to be built after the Second World War. Despite the title, the focus is much more on von Neumann than on Turing.

Walter Isaacson's *The Innovators: How a Group of Hackers, Geniuses, and Geeks Created the Digital Revolution* gives a wide, sweeping history of the computer starting with Babbage and ending with the Web.

Computers, minds, and the universe

Scott Aaronson, David Deutsch, and Douglas Hofstadter are three computer scientists who have written thought-provoking works on a wide variety of ideas related to the theory of computation. *Quantum Computing since Democritus* by Aaranson, *The Beginning of Infinity: Explanations That Transform the World* by Deutsch, and *Gödel, Escher, Bach* by Hofstadter are all fascinating.

Cellular automata

We only looked briefly looked at cellular automata, but they have a long and interesting history. They were first studied by Ulam and von Neumann as the first computers were built. Nils Barricelli was at Princeton during the 1950s and used the computer to simulate the interaction of cells. George Dyson's *Turing's Cathedral* gives a good historical description of this work

John Conway, in 1970, defined *Life* involving two-dimensional cellular automata. These were popularized by Martin Gardner in *Scientific American*. William Poundstone's *The Recursive Universe* is a good book on the history of these automata and how complexity can arise from simple rules. (This book was first published in 1985, but was been republished by Dover Press in 2013.)

Stephen Wolfram's *A New Kind of Science* is an encyclopedia of one-dimensional cellular automata with extensive notes.

Theory of computation

A.K. Dewdney's *The New Turing Omnibus* contains sixty six short chapters. Each chapter is a short article on some important part of theoretical computer science. It contains a wealth of information on a wide variety of topics. It is highly recommended for someone who wants to learn more about theoretical computer science.

There are now a number of good texts on the theory of computation that are aimed at undergraduate computer science and mathematics majors. However, these tend to be expensive and are meant to complement a course with an instructor. That said, a good modern textbook is *Introduction to the Theory of Computation* by Michael Sipser.

A classic, somewhat older, but excellent text, is *Introduction to Automata Theory Languages and Computation* by John Hopcroft and Jeffrey Ullman.

There are also a number of online courses. ADUni.org has one that is excellent.

Notes

Introduction

1. Turing didn't name these machines after himself. He called them *a*-machines, which stood for automatic machine. It was Alonzo Church who first called them Turing machines, and the name stuck.

2. This is in the Preface of Minsky's *Computation: Finite and Infinite Machines.*

Chapter 1

1. Bertrand Russell. *Mysticism and Logic: And Other Essays* p.60.

2. We will use postulates and axioms interchangeably. Euclid did distinguish between the two terms. His starting point was a list of axioms and a separate list of postulates. Nowadays we would combine the two lists and just call them axioms.

3. Bertrand Russell. *Recent Work on the Principles of Mathematics* p. 83.

4. John Henry Ketcham. *The Life of Abraham Lincoln* p.62.

5. We give a taste of how Boolean algebra works.
   The truth tables connected to *and*, $\wedge$, and *or*, $\vee$ are:

   $$T \wedge T = T, \quad T \wedge F = F, \quad F \wedge T = F, \quad F \wedge F = F,$$

   and

   $$T \vee T = T, \quad T \vee F = T, \quad F \vee T = T, \quad F \vee F = F.$$

   It is standard to associate T with 1 and F with 0. Boolean algebra gives a way of using algebra to do logic. For example, *and* can be represented by multiplication, $\times$. The statement $X \wedge Y$ becomes $X \times Y$. The truth table for *and* is described simply by

   $$1 \times 1 = 1, \quad 1 \times 0 = 0, \quad 0 \times 1 = 0, \quad 0 \times 0 = 0.$$

For *or*, the statement $X \vee Y$ can be represented by $X + Y - X \times Y$. (It is straightforward to check that we get the correct appropriate truth table.)

The negation of a statement P is denoted by $\neg P$. In Boolean algebra, $\neg X$ is given by $1 - X$, which just says that if $X = 1$ then $\neg X = 0$ and that if $X = 0$ then $\neg X = 1$.

With these preliminaries out of the way it is possible to derive the basic logical identities using algebra. We will just give one example. The statement $\neg(P \vee Q)$ means exactly the same thing as $(\neg P) \wedge (\neg Q)$. (This is one of DeMorgan's laws.) We will show the equivalence of $\neg(X \vee Y)$ and $\neg X \wedge \neg Y$ using algebra.

First note that $\neg(X \vee Y)$ corresponds to $1 - (X + Y - X \times Y)$ and $\neg X \wedge \neg Y$ corresponds to $(1 - X) \times (1 - Y)$. Simple algebra shows that both of these equal $1 - X - Y + X \times Y$, and so the two statements are equivalent.

6. As the American philosopher, mathematician, and computer scientist, Hilary Putnam, writes in the article "Peirce the Logician":

> While, to my knowledge, no one except Frege ever published a single paper in Frege's notation, many famous logicians adopted Peirce-Schröder notation, and famous results and systems were published in it.
>
> ....
>
> Frege did "discover" the quantifier in the sense of having the rightful claim to priority; but Peirce and his students discovered it in the effective sense. The fact is that until Russell appreciated what he had done, Frege was relatively obscure, and it was Peirce who seems to have been known to the entire world logical community. How many of the people who think that "Frege invented logic" are aware of these facts?

7. The machine is now owned by the Museum of the History of Science in Oxford.

8. T. S. Eliot. "Commentary," *The Monthly Criterion*, October 1927, p. 291.

9. Algorithms are step by step procedures for performing computations. The word "algorithm" comes from the Latin translation of

Al-Khwarizmi, a Persian mathematician, who around 850 C.E. wrote the book *On the Calculation with Hindu Numerals*. This book introduced among other things our standard decimal notation for numbers. Though algorithms are named after Al-Khwarizmi the idea has always been part of mathematics. Euclid's *Elements* contains the *Euclidean Algorithm* for finding the greatest common divisor of two positive integers, but even earlier, around 1600 B.C.E., the Babylonians developed algorithms for finding square roots.

10. Andrew Hodges. *Alan Turing: The Enigma* p. 120.

11. Saint Augustine warned that Christians should beware of *mathematici*. He was warning about astrologers, not what we now refer to as mathematicians!

Chapter 2

1. This treatment is now called electroconvulsive therapy and is usually administered with muscle relaxants. In Post's time, muscle relaxants were not used. Electroshock resulted in whole body convulsions. Post died of a heart attack shortly after receiving his last electroshock at the age of fifty seven.

2. In fact, there are no positive integer solutions to $x^n + y^n = z^n$ when n is larger than 2. This is the famous Fermat's Last Theorem. Fermat wrote the statement in the margin of a book with the comment that he had a marvelous proof, but that the margin wasn't large enough for him to include it. In 1994, 357 years later, Andrew Wiles finally proved it. Most mathematicians don't believe that Fermat had a legitimate proof. The result should be more properly called Fermat's conjecture or Wiles's theorem.

3. All three of the problems we looked at have the property that there was an algorithm that works in the case when the answer of the decision problem was yes, but not in the case when the answer was no. Problems like this, where there is an algorithm for the *Yes* case, but not for the *No* case are sometimes called partially decidable, but not decidable (or recursively enumerable, but not recursive).

Chapter 3

1. Wiener wrote the classic book *Cybernetics, or Control and Communication in the Animal and the Machine* in 1948.

2. Later von Neumann wrote a wide-ranging paper, "The general and logical theory of automata," and from this time on, theoretical models of computers became known as automata.

3. ASCII was invented in 1963 and became the standard way of encoding in the English speaking part of the world for many years. However, it is only possible to encode $2^7 = 128$ characters with seven bits. Different countries had letters and symbols that were not included in the standard ASCII and so had to modify the coding for their use. As the internet and the World Wide Web grew, it became important to extend the encoding in a consistent way, with each encoded string meaning the same thing all over the world. Currently, the new standard is Unicode. This is a list that assigns characters and symbols to numbers of which the first 128 agree with ASCII. The list keeps being updated is still growing. As of June 2015, the list contains just over a million entries and includes one hundred twenty nine different writing scripts.

4. A parity check is sometimes built into bar codes. These are often designed so that readers can read the code both right-side up and upside down. The parity check is used for determining which way up the strip is being read or, equivalently, whether the strip is being read from left to right or from right to left.

5. The second part of the proof usually involves converting regular expressions to non-deterministic automata and then showing that non-deterministic automata have exactly the same computational power as deterministic ones. This is not difficult, and is done in the standard undergraduate course, but it is a little too lengthy to include here.

6. *Mastering Regular Expressions* by Jeffrey Friedl is one example of a popular book that explicitly shows the usefulness of regular expressions in a variety of practical applications.

7. What are known as 'office mailboxes' in the United States are commonly known 'pigeonholes' in the United Kingdom.

8. We will only be looking at two types of automata; finite automata and Turing machines. In a standard course on the theory of computation it is usual to also study pushdown automata, a class of machines that is more computationally powerful that finite automata, but less powerful than Turing machines. The examples concerning equal numbers of 0s and 1s and balanced brackets can be tackled by pushdown automata. A question that is beyond pushdown automata is looking at strings using an alphabet of three letters and asking whether the strings have the same number of each letter.

Chapter 4

1. Alan Turing. "Computing machinery and intelligence."

2. Below is the complete computation when the Turing machine TM_2 is run on the string

$$(\quad (\quad) \quad).$$

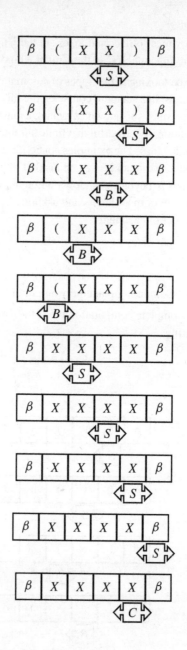

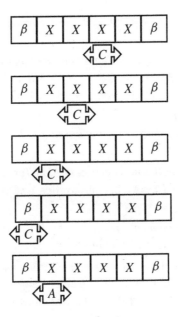

3. Leibniz's notation is the standard $\frac{dx}{dt}$ notation for the derivative of x with respect to t. This is denoted by $\dot{x}$ in Newton's notation.

4. Introduction to Wittgenstein's *Tractatus*.

5. This is not a trivial fact. In 1985, David Deutsch, one of the pioneers of this area, published a landmark paper in quantum computation, "Quantum theory, the Church-Turing principle and the universal quantum computer." In this paper he described quantum computers and how they differed from conventional computers. The question was whether quantum computers were more computationally powerful than traditional computers. It took some time, but the conclusion was that they were not.

Chapter 5

1. There were different versions of this machine. Two versions have been constructed from Babbage's designs. One is on display at the London Science Museum. The other is owned by Nathan Myhrvold

and is currently on display at the Computer History Museum in California.

2. *Sketch of The Analytical Engine Invented by Charles Babbage By L. F. MENABREA of Turin, Officer of the Military Engineers With notes upon the Memoir by the Translator ADA AUGUSTA, COUNTESS OF LOVELACE.*

3. David Deutsch. *The Beginning of Infinity: Explanations That Transform the World.*

4. This appears in the introduction to *Alan Turing's Systems of Logic: The Princeton Thesis.* This introduction is also available on Appel's website.

5. Hermann Grassmann's book *Lehrbuch der Arithmetik für höhere Lehranstalten* can be found in The Internet Archive.

6. The lambda in the λ-calculus evolved from notation used by Russell and Whitehead. They used $\hat{x}$. Church felt that the symbol $\hat{}$ should come before the x and should be written as $\hat{}x$. This then got typeset as λx.

7. The function $+$ takes two numbers as input and gives a number as output. In the λ-calculus, $+$ is usually written first, so instead of writing $m + n$, you write $+(m)(n)$, which, though it looks strange, makes it clear that $+$ is a function with two inputs. If this notation is used, then $+$ is defined by $+ \equiv \lambda mnsx.ms(nsx)$.

8. As with $+$, $\wedge$ is a function with two inputs. Instead of writing $T \wedge F$, you write $\wedge(T)(F)$.

9. Post used the term *tag* because this process of letters "running" from one end of the sting to the other reminded him of the children's game tag.

10. Marvin Minsky did considerable research on these systems. His book *Computation: Finite and infinite machines* is an excellent resource.

11. Liesbeth De Mol, "Tag Systems and Collatz-like functions." *Theoretical Computer Science*, vol. 390, 2008, pp. 92–101.

12. The calculation starts with a number n represented by a string of n as. As we apply the tag system the as get replaced by a string of

alternating bs and cs. During this first phase we are removing aa from the front of the string and adding bc to the end, so the length of the string remains constant with n terms in it. There are now two cases to consider depending on whether the initial number n is even or add.

If the initial number of as is even, after the tag system has run through all of the as, the resulting string contains alternating bs and cs. It begins with a b and ends with a c. For the next $n/2$ iterations, the system removes a bc from the beginning of the string and adds an a to the end. This means that the length of the string decreases by one for each iteration. After the system has run through all the bs it will consist of a string of as with length $n - n/2$ which is equal to $n/2$.

If the initial number of as is odd, after the tag system has run through all of the as, the resulting string contains alternating bs and cs. It both begins and ends with a c. This means that the string has $(n + 1)/2$ cs. For each of the next $(n + 1)/2$ iterations the tag system removes a cb from the front of the string and adds aaa to the end. This means that the length of the string increases by one for each iteration. After the system has run through all the cs it will consist of a string of as with length $n + (n + 1)/2$ which is equal to $(3n + 1)/2$.

13. Matthew Cook, "Universality in Elementary Cellular Automata." *Complex Systems*, 15 (2004) 1-40.

Chapter 6

1. These machines were first introduced by Stephen Cook and Robert Reckhow in 1973.

2. This requires that the integer in R_s is non-negative.

3. A key idea in the conversion is dealing with the information on the tapes. The information on each of the tapes is copied to the machine with one tape. A new symbol, # say, is used to separate the copies of the tapes. We have to deal with each tape having its own head. The

way this is done is by taking each letter in the alphabet and inventing a modified version of it. If 0 is in the alphabet, then we might invent $\hat{0}$. This new symbol will let the new machine know where the head for that tape is located. For example if we had two tapes, with *abbaaa* written on the first tape with its head at the first *b*, and 010101 written on a second tape with its head at the second 0, we would encode this as

$$\#a\hat{b}baaa\#01\hat{0}101\#.$$

The rest of the conversion is tedious, but the important point is that it can be done.

4. Minsky's book *Computation: Finite and Infinite Machines* contains a wealth of information about Tag systems.

5. Cook's representation simulates Turing machines in exponential time. Turlogh Neary and Damien Woods in 2006 gave a different way of representing Turing machines by *Rule 110* that only takes polynomial time [35]. This implies that any problem that can be solved in polynomial time by a Turing machine can be solved in polynomial time by *Rule 110*.

6. Randall Munroe draws the webcomic "xkcd." The comic "A bunch of rocks" features *Rule 110* and the creation of the universe.

7. The author thanks an anonymous referee for suggesting this example.

8. In the real world compilers are often written in the language they compile. This process is called *bootstrapping*. The first compiler of a new language is written using some other language, but subsequent compilers are usually written in the language being compiled. This raises interesting questions concerning the trust you can have that the compiled version of your program will run correctly.

   If you write a new compiler, to be absolutely sure that it is correct, it is not enough to just check your program, but you need to know that the compiler that is compiling it is trustworthy. It is possible that the original compiler could insert a *Trojan horse* into the compiled versions of subsequent compilers. Ken Thompson, one of the main designers of UNIX, brought this to public attention when he discussed this in his acceptance speech for the Turing Award in 1983.[1]

Chapter 7

1. The Greek classical philosophers used this technique in many of their arguments. In this context it is usually referred to as *reductio ad absurdum*.

2. It actually comes from *quoziente*, the Italian word for quotient. It was invented by Giuseppe Peano, the Italian mathematician, who first used the notation in 1895.

3. This definition is not quite correct. We want $1/2$, $2/4$ and $17/34$ all to denote the same number. The way that we have currently defined the rationals makes it look as though they are all different numbers. This shouldn't cause us any problems, but strictly we should define an *equivalence relation* and then define the rational numbers to be *equivalence classes* — $1/2$, $2/4$ and $17/34$ all belonging to the same equivalence class.

4. Another way of describing undecidability is in terms of languages associated to Turing machines. If the complement of a Turing machine's language is also the language of a Turing machine, then the language is decidable. Decidable languages correspond to decidable problems. The observation in the chapter on finite automata that the complement of a regular language is also a regular language implies that all regular languages are decidable. Decidable languages are often called *recursive*. Languages of Turing machines on the whole are called *recursively enumerable*. The set of recursively enumerable languages includes the recursive languages.

---

1 "Reflections on Trusting Trust" was presented by Ken Thompson in 1983. It was published in the *Communications of the ACM* and is widely available on the web.

5. It is known that $S(2) = 6$. Here is a machine that, given a blank input tape, takes six steps until it halts.

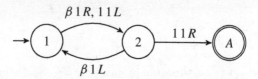

Here's the compuation:

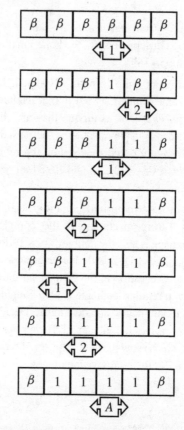

6. Scott Aaronson's webpage lists several of his articles. One of these, *Who Can Name the Bigger Number*, concerns $S(n)$. It is well-worth reading.

7. Martin Davis was a student of Post as an undergraduate, a student of Church for his graduate work, and an assistant of Shannon for awhile. He won several prizes for his work on Hilbert's tenth problem for which he contributed an essential part of the proof that this problem is undecidable.

   He is also a great expositor. His *Computability and Unsolvability*, first published in 1958, was the first text that discussed the theory of computation based around Turing machines. This book presented ideas that had been only in the domain of logicians in a way that made them much more comprehensible to computer scientists.

Chapter 8

1. The set A is *contained* in the set B if every element of A is an element of B. The set A is *strictly contained* in B if A is contained in B, but there is at least one element of B that is not in A. Every element of A belongs to B, but there are some elements of B that do not belong to A.

2. Aleph, $\aleph$, is the first letter of the Hebrew alphabet.

3. It is based on the assumption that if both $|A| \leq |B|$ and $|B| \leq |A|$ then $|A| = |B|$. This, though true, is not obvious for infinite sets. The result is a consequence of a famous result called the Schröder-Bernstein theorem.

4. The reader may have met this idea when looking at limits in calculus. The forms $\infty - \infty$ and ∞/∞ are called indeterminate forms. Limits involving indeterminate forms have to be analyzed carefully.

Chapter 9

1. The actual quote is from a talk Dijkstra gave at a conference in 1984: "The Fathers of the field had been pretty confusing: John von Neumann speculated about computers and the human brain in analogies sufficiently wild to be worthy of a medieval thinker and Alan

M. Turing thought about criteria to settle the question of whether Machines Can Think, a question of which we now know that it is about as relevant as the question of whether Submarines Can Swim."

2. Andrew Hodges. *Op. cit.*, p. 167.

3. Martin Davis. *The Universal Computer: The Road from Leibniz to Turing*, p. 169.

4. Since Turing was a student of Church, he adopted the λ-calculus to express the ideas. Unfortunately, this made the work somewhat hard to read and probably explains why it hasn't been widely read.

5. "Symbolic Analysis of Relay and Switching Circuits," *Transactions American Institute of Electrical Engineers*, vol. 57, 1938.

6. This later was renamed as Government Communications Headquarters, but is more well known by the acronym GCHQ. It is the British equivalent to the American NSA.

7. The English "bombe" was named after the Polish "bomba." Why the Poles called their machine bomba (which translates as bomb in English) seems to be a mystery. Rejewksi, when asked about this, is said to have replied that he couldn't think of a better name.

8. Both Shannon and Turing were interested in using ideas from probability to extract information from data. Shannon would later extend some of his wartime work and write the groundbreaking paper "A Mathematical Theory of Communication" that is one of the foundations of *Information Theory*. Turing wrote several articles on the application of probability to cryptography. These were classified and only now are being made available to the public (two papers were declassified in 2012. They are available at http://www.nationalarchives.gov.uk).

9. The English use the term *valve* where the Americans use *vacuum tube*.

10. The National Museum of Computing in Bletchley Park has reconstructed a Colossus. Visitors can see the machine running.

11. OBE stands for the Officer of the Order of the British Empire. This is a couple of levels down from a knighthood.

12. Mauchly and Eckert went to court several times trying to obtain patents, but were never successful.

13. Andrew Hodges. *Op. cit.*, p. 382.

14. George Dyson. *Turing's Cathedral*, p. ix.

15. In 1990, Hugh Loebner pledged $100,000 in prize money and a gold medal for the first computer to pass the Turing test. Each year since 1991 there has been a competition and a bronze medal and prize money is awarded for the "most human-like" computer.

16. Scott Aaronson. *Quantum Computing Since Democritus*, p. 45.

17. This was reported in the *Daily Telegraph* on June 18, 1954. Both the biographies by Hodges and Copeland include this quote.

Bibliography

[1] Aaronson, Scott. *Quantum Computing Since Democritus*, Cambridge University Press, 2013.

[2] Appel, Andrew W. *Alan Turing's Systems of Logic: The Princeton Thesis*, Princeton University Press; Reprint edition (November 16, 2014).

[3] Boole, George. *An Investigation of the Laws of Thought: on which are founded the mathematical theories of logic and probabilities*, (1854). Available from Project Gutenberg (https://www.gutenberg.org).

[4] Church, Alonzo. "A Note on the Entscheidungsproblem," *Journal of Symbolic Logic*, 1, pp. 40–41, 1936.

[5] Cohen, Paul. "The Independence of the Continuum Hypothesis," *Proceedings of the National Academy of Sciences of the United States of America* 50 (6): pp.1143–1148, 1964.

[6] Cook, Matthew. "Universality in Elementary Cellular Automata," *Complex Systems*, 15, 2004, pp. 1–40.

[7] Cook, S. A; Reckhow, R. A. "Time bounded random access machines," *J. Computer and Systems Sciences* 7:4, 1973, pp. 343–353.

[8] Copeland, B. Jack. *The Essential Turing*, Oxford University Press, 2004.

[9] Copeland, B. Jack. *Turing: Pioneer of the Information Age*, Oxford University Press, 2012.

[10] Davis, Martin. *Computability and Unsolvability*, reprinted by Dover, 1985.

[11] Davis, Martin. *The Universal Computer: The Road from Leibniz to Turing*, W. W. Norton & Company, 2000.

[12] De Mol, Liesbeth. "Tag systems and Collatz-like functions," *Theoretical Computer Science*, vol. 390, 2008, pp. 92–101.

[13] Deutsch, David. *The Beginning of Infinity: Explanations That Transform the World*, Penguin Books; Reprint edition. 2012.

[14] Deutsch, David. "Quantum theory, the Church-Turing principle and the universal quantum computer," *Proceedings of the Royal Society of London* A 400, 1985, pp. 97–117.

[15] Dewdney, A. K. *The (New) Turing Omnibus*, Holt, 1993.

[16] Dyson, George. *Turing's Cathedral*, Pantheon Books, 2012.

[17] Eliot, T.S. "Commentary," *The Monthly Criterion*, October 1927.

[18] Euclid (Based on T. L. Heath's Translation). *Euclid's Elements: All thirteen books in one volume*, reprinted by Green Lion Press, 2002.

[19] Friedl, Jeffrey. *Mastering Regular Expressions*, O'Reilly Media; Third Edition edition, 2006.

[20] Gamow, George. *One Two Three . . . Infinity: Facts and Speculations of Science*, Dover, 1988.

[21] Gödel, Kurt. *Collected Works: Volume I: Publications 1929–1936*, edited by Solomon Feferman et. al. Oxford University Press, 1986.

[22] Goldstine, Herman H. *The Computer from Pascal to von Neumann*, Princeton University Press, 1972.

[23] Hilbert, David. *The Foundations of Geometry*, Chicago: Open Court, 2nd Edition, 1980 (1899).

[24] Hodges, Andrew. *Alan Turing: The Enigma*, Princeton University Press, reprinted in 2014.

[25] Hofstadter, Douglas R. *Gödel, Escher, Bach: An Eternal Golden Braid*, Basic Books, 1979.

[26] Hofstadter, Douglas R. *I Am a Strange Loop*, Basic Books, 2007.

[27] Hopcroft, John; Ullman, Jeffrey. *Introduction to Automata Theory, Languages and Computation*, Addison-Wesley, 1979.

[28] Isaacson, Walter. *The Innovators: How a Group of Hackers, Geniuses, and Geeks Created the Digital Revolution*, Simon & Schuster, 2014.

[29] Ketcham, John Henry. *The Life of Abraham Lincoln*, reprinted by Forgotten Books, 2008.

[30] McCulloch, Warren S; Pitts, Walter H. "A Logical Calculus of Ideas Immanent in Nervous Activity," *Bulletin of Mathematical Biophysics*, Vol. 5, 1943, pp. 115–133.

[31] Menabrea, Luigi; Lovelace, Ada. *Sketch of the Analytical Engine Invented by Charles Babbage By L. F. MENABREA of Turin, Officer of the Military Engineers With Notes upon the Memoir by the Translator ADA AUGUSTA, COUNTESS OF LOVELACE* Scientific Memoirs, Vol 3 (1842).

[32] Minsky, Marvin. *Computation: Finite and Infinite Machines*, Prentice-Hall, 1967.

[33] Minsky, Marvin; Papert, Seymour. *Perceptrons: An Introduction to Computational Geometry, Expanded Edition*, Cambridge, MA: MIT Press, 1988.

[34] Nagel, Ernest; Newman, James; Hofstadter, Douglas R. *Gödel's Proof*, NYU Press, Revised Edition, 2001.

[35] Neary, Turlogh; Woods, Damien. "P-completeness of Cellular Automaton Rule 110," *Automata, Languages and Programming*, Lecture Notes in Computer Science Volume 4051, 2006, pp 132–143.

[36] Petzold, Charles. *The Annotated Turing*, Wiley, 2008.

[37] Poundstone, William. *The Recursive Universe: Cosmic Complexity and the Limits of Scientific Knowledge*, reprinted by Dover, 2013.

[38] Putnam, Hillary. "Peirce the Logician," *Historia Mathematica* 9: pp. 290–301, 1982.

[39] Rosenblatt, Frank. "The Perceptron: A Probalistic Model for Information Storage and Organization in the Brain," *Psychological Review* 65 (6): 386–408, 1958.

[40] Rumelhart, David E.; McClelland, James. *Parallel Distributed Processing: Explorations in the Microstructure of Cognition*, Cambridge: MIT Press, 1986.

[41] Russell, Bertrand. *Mysticism and Logic: And other Essays*, Longmans, Green and Company, 1919.

[42] Russell, Bertrand; Whitehead, Alfred North. *Principia Mathematica*, Cambridge University Press, Second Edition, 1963.

[43] Russell, Bertrand. "Recent Work on the Principles of Mathematics," *International Monthly* 4, 1901, pp. 83–101.

[44] Shannon, Claude. "Symbolic Analysis of Relay and Switching Circuits," *Transactions American Institute of Electrical Engineers*, vol. 57, 1938, pp. 38–80.

[45] Sipser, Michael. *Introduction to the Theory of Computation*, Cengage Learning, 2012.

[46] Soare, Robert. "Formalism and intuition in computability," *Phil. Trans. R, soc.* A, (2012) 370, pp. 3277–3304.

[47] Thompson, Ken. "Reflections on Trusting Trust," *Communications of the ACM*, August 1984, vol. 27, no. 8, pp. 761–763.

[48] Tibor, Radó. "On non-computable functions," *Bell System Technical Journal* 41 (3) pp. 877–884, 1962.

[49] Turing, Alan. "Computing machinery and intelligence," *Mind* 1950, 59, 433–460.

[50] Turing, Alan. "On Computable Numbers, with an Application to the Entscheidungsproblem," *Proceedings of the London Mathematical Society*, Series 2, 42 (1936–7), pp. 230–265.

[51] von Neumann, John. "First Draft of a Report on the EDVAC," reprinted in *IEEE Annals of the History of Computing*, Vol. 15, 1993.

[52] von Neumann, John. *Collected Works: Volume V*. Pergamon Press, 1961.

[53] Wiener, Norbert. *Cybernetics, or Control and Communication in the Animal and the Machine*. Cambridge: MIT Press, 1961.

[54] Wolfram, Stephen. *A New Kind of Science*. Wolfram Media, 2002.

Index